IS THIS LOVE?

A Guide to Loving Relationships for Teenagers,
From the Reflections of a Teenager

Charley Sky Gardner

*This book is dedicated to all the women who
told me I had something worth saying.*

CONTENTS

PREFACE

The reason that humans are able to have deeply meaningful connections that surpass the standard model of animal love is our access to imagination. We as a race have the ability to see beyond: to fathom the unfathomable, to reach for more than just the necessities of survival. This gift is accompanied by a greed for sublimity. In such a way, imagination —thinking that deviates from the basic needs of life—leads to an abundance of unique experiences and forms of love. This is what makes us human. We are hardwired to need to reach for more, to imagine the best of what could be, but no one teaches us how to actually *use* our imagination to our benefit. We may be able to want more, but there is no definitive roadmap to knowing what that is we feel that yearning for. Of course we can imagine love, but who is there to tell us the *way* to love or be loved?

I grew up with two very devoted divorced parents. Like many children of divorced parents, I was packing my bags every weekend to go from one house to another and doing the math on how many holidays I would spend in either place. When my parents did find themselves trying to put the pieces back together, I found myself sitting at the top of the stairs waiting for them to stop fighting about one thing or another. Despite the fact that they both shared so much love for each other, shouting matches and tears frequently replaced family time. So, as this was all I had known, to me a healthy relationship was defined by distress and conflict. It made sense that a family argued and yelled at each other every single day. I didn't question, is this love? Although unbeknownst to me, this had been setting me up for a narrow worldview in which hate and love were set to coexist in a home.

Each was inconceivable without the presence of the other.

It wasn't until my father remarried that my perception of love widened. After a childhood of watching hurt and desperation, I grew up clinging onto any promising affection in my relationships outside the house. Unfortunately, those promises were the illusions of pieces I felt were missing from my life, and in them I found no salvation. I began unknowingly trying to fill the gaps from my childhood through relationships, and my blindness led me nowhere but deeper into my own pain. I fell victim to my own warped reality; I did not know how to be loved and I didn't know how to love. I—or rather what was subconsciously my childhood self—started dating people that resembled the attributes I recognized in my parents. There is a poem, "Starved," by author Lauren Eden, that I am always brought back to, in which she writes, "When you are not fed love on a silver spoon you learn to lick it off knives." All children grow up seeking love, and regardless of how kind or painful a form that takes, we get accustomed to receiving that love in any way possible. We have no other choice as little ones: to be loved is always the way to survive.

Watching my father remarry changed my conscious expectation for connection. I observed him and his new partner as they grew and learned together, never remaining seated in the past, consistently improving themselves not just for the other, but also for themselves. I saw how they listened to one another and *heard* each other, especially when it was something that they didn't want to hear. And the hearing was not just through one ear and out the other, they internalized it. They *felt* one another through their words. The relationship was never just about one person. It was a harmony of recognized, respected equality: a genuine alchemy.

All throughout my childhood, regardless of the state of our family, my father always urged compassion. If I got into an argument on the playground, he would ask me something along the lines of, "Well, why do you think *they* were upset?" He never invalidated my feelings or made them seem like a weakness, but he always encouraged me to put myself in the other person's position. Even now, if I'm having difficulties with someone else he asks me first, "How do you imagine they felt?" By planting this little seedling of a thought he taught me to use our uniquely human gift, our imagination, to intentionally understand both myself and others. He always prompted me to search for what's underneath as a pathway to compassion and greater connection. Through teaching me to expand my perspective outside of myself, my father showed me that another person's anger or sadness was something that I too could understand, not just react to. And moreover that those visible emotions tended to mask something more tender like loneliness, despondency, loss, and most delicately, fear.

Through my exploration of the different facets of relationships, I have met with love in joy and in pain. I've intersected with love, lust, infatuation, and heartbreak, and I've also discovered what it means to have home be not a place but a person. In any case, this book won't have all the answers. It can't— me and the philosophers, along with the poets, are still searching for them every single day. However, after much trial and error, I've done my best to do justice to the ways of love. Being only 15 when I first began writing this book, I knew that my experience was limited, but that very fact is what I believe to be the key to any insight I may offer. The feelings of what it's like to experience our first romantic relationships are fresh in my mind. The excitement, confusion, intensity, and heartbreak are immediately tangible to me in a way they wouldn't be if I wrote this book ten years from now. At this moment I feel exactly what you feel.

Relationships are intricate, but they're not impossible to understand. With intention and patience, they reveal themselves to be incredibly worthwhile. In this book we will start from the beginning, before the relationship itself even begins. We will first look inwards to ourselves, then go through love, and in the end, breach the surface, learning how to let go, or how to make sure we never have to.

CHAPTER 1: WHAT DOES A HEALTHY RELATIONSHIP LOOK LIKE?

Snowflakes are arranged in minute hexagonal structures. Although these structures all have the same origin, each is invariably unique from any other—as are we, as are our relationships. We all begin as the same tiny little organisms bobbing around, then over the course of our development we acquire our values, preferences, fears, passions, love languages, and our stories.

While every relationship looks different, there needs to exist the presence of four main principles in order to maintain a sustainable, thriving connection. They are: growth, empathy, communication, and forgiveness. These not only make your relationships healthier, but they allow a safe space of trust to be cultivated within them. Although this may seem to be second nature, in the midst of love, our own personal feelings intrude upon our relationships, of course. They must, inherently, be intrusive as love is the closest we may get to ourselves. A conversation, for example, about how much time you spend together seems simple in theory, until you both disagree entirely and the barriers to understanding each other push you further apart. On account of the fact that in a relationship both people have their own perspectives and understandings of the world, relationships take immense effort and work, where it is necessary for both partners to want to put in that work.

There then cannot be one right way to be in a partnership with someone else. In the same way, being that we all have these different facets of ourselves, a strong relationship cannot just be about one person. It is, though, an ill-famed idea that relationships are meant to be 50/50. There will very rarely be a time when all members of a relationship are giving or receiving 100% because outside of our relationship, we are still leading our own lives.

The scale tips, because we are all human and none of us are capable of perfect, precise happiness at all times. We need to be comfortable with how naturally asymmetrical the balance of relationships is. However, when the scale becomes perpetually unbalanced and never reverts, one partner ends up giving more energy to a relationship without receiving the same dedication back. As a consequence, the congruous nature of the relationship cedes. One person should never be fully responsible for taking care of the other in perpetuity: that is the job of a parent, not a lover. Balance does mean every partner is always giving their all, but their "all," so to say, will always look different. If one partner is overwhelmed by stressful deadlines, their "all" may be an, "I love you. How was your day?" When done out of love, the weight of something small is equal to that of something large.

Part of putting in the work in a relationship means being able to handle conflict. A common misconception is that a healthy relationship means never having conflict, moreover than having any conflict at all means your relationship is doomed to fail. However, the truth is that conflict is essential for growth. You and your partner are bound to argue. Being under the misapprehension that conflict is unnatural will inevitably harm your relationships; you will reactively detach as soon as a problem arises. Your partner is one of the chief components of your life, naturally what they say and do impacts you much more than other people. What matters, though, is how you two can handle conflict together.

Now, there is a difference between productive conflict and harmful fighting, which may appear interchangeable when trying to differentiate. If you and your partner are unable to maintain a difficult conversation without extreme turbulence (from one or both sides), there is a lack of something, whether that be trust, readiness, or self-regulation. Likewise, if you cannot discuss something outside of the exciting euphoria with the absence of taking a defensive stance, there is a disconnect somewhere (a topic we'll delve into further down).

One of the biggest indicators of an unsound relationship is when nothing important can be brought to attention. There are two dimensions to this issue, the first being arguing solely about the more minute matters to avoid the real issues in the relationship. Frustration over a bland text, miscommunication, or getting a date wrong often reflects something more important that is being left unsaid. The second is avoiding important topics as a way to avoid cultivating a more serious relationship. It is invaluable to keep communicating with one another, otherwise the little nuances amalgamate and consume your relationship.

A less conscious source of turbulence in a relationship is the fact that everyone has different wants and expectations in a relationship—things they value dearly that their partner may not care much about or have even thought about before. This is where empathy and communication come in. No one should assume their partner will automatically know how to treat them. We teach others how to love us, just as they teach us to care for them. To look at it another way, an author should not be upset that the reader disagrees with the actions of the characters before he or she knows their backstories. Initially, the reader may only consider the characters' decisions from their own viewpoint, derived only as projections from their own experiences in real life. The fiction is first only a reflection of the reader, before they might step out of their own world and into the one created by the writer.

In one of my past relationships, with someone who we'll refer to as Riley, Riley valued consistent talking and calling much more than I did. I didn't care much for it, but for Riley it was a characterizable sign of love. When I didn't reach out as much as he did, he felt overlooked and separate from my list of priorities. Luckily, Riley felt comfortable enough with me to tell me how he felt. I was able to listen open-mindedly, realizing he was not attacking my behavior but rather simply needed more consistent communication than I did. So, I chose to make a change. I created time to text and call him every day, despite the fact that I didn't receive the same sense of comfort from it as he did.

In relationships, to internalize every little thing is to sabotage yourself. If you were walking down the street and some passerby looked at you with an angry expression, you of course wouldn't take that to heart. Perhaps they missed their bus or spilled their morning coffee. You'd understand it had nothing to do with you, you were just a passerby who, on a whim, received the blunt of their unhappiness. Even though I cared for Riley just as much as he cared for me, I was not a very talkative person at the time. Riley's need for communication had less to do with me and more to do with some of his own anxieties. If he hadn't explained the importance of it to me, I would have never noticed the disparity. Like you and the hypothetical passerby, if I had taken the situation to heart we would've just started fighting for no reason. It wasn't my fault he was upset, but by noticing and listening I was able to help him feel more at ease.

It wasn't just necessary that we talked about it with one another, but that we really tried to feel what the other was feeling. He must have felt a sense of rejection when I didn't want to talk as consistently as he did. This thus became a shared weight, because, even if entirely by accident, it meant I had done something to hurt him. I could've disengaged to make myself feel more secure, but instead of feeling attacked, I looked at it from his perspective. It is unbelievably tempting to try and disregard something that hands you guilt, even more so in the face of love. This is exactly when it is most paramount to take a breath and hear what your partner is trying to say to you. They really only want to be *heard* by you.

To listen is one of the great secrets to thriving relationships. Oftentimes your partner (or friend, or parent) is not looking for you to fix the problem, give advice, or even *help* them at all—only for them to know you're acknowledging what they're feeling. Sometimes, your partner's complaints may seem small, but if it matters to them it is, as a result, now important to you. Empathy and communication go hand in hand and one does not exist well without the other. Listening without judgment is easier than just hearing what's said. Empathy becomes most valuable when you don't understand your partner, or when you find yourself at odds with their perspective. A relationship is a pair of consciousnesses with emotions and opinions that both deserve to be recognized. We don't have to take responsibility for all of our partner's feelings, but we have to embrace them as if they are our own.

Everyone we engage with, romantically or not, has gone through something in their lives that affects their present relationships. We are made up of our experiences, we all have triggers, and when they come up it is important to be patient with those trying to take care of us. In a solid relationship, both individuals can hold space for one another. This means letting the other hurt without distorting the focus to themselves and eclipsing the other's distress, and instead just recognizing their pain. If your partner is expressing their pain or frustration to you, even if you don't understand it at all, doing your best to just hear it and be overly curious to fully understand them makes all the difference.

At the same time, the expectation in a healthy relationship is that the other partner is actively trying to reprogram themselves. Part of human development is the process of evolving from our early stages of life, which involves growing out of the influences and experiences of our past. Letting go is one of the most difficult things a person can do. Holding space for someone to do that is just as difficult. Growing is arduous. It is like being asked all of a sudden to switch from your native language to a foreign one, never having been taught how to speak that language, and it never ends. We learn one thing and it burns into our mind and then we discover it is wrong and then we have to do it all over again. Once we master one vernacular, another spontaneously arises. We reprogram that and suddenly realize that didn't make sense either, so then we have to reprogram that again and so on and so on. It is never-ending and in a relationship it takes two to really handle it. It is uncomfortable to grow, therefore when two people decide to undergo it together—to walk through a strange, unfamiliar world hand in hand—the result is a bond more powerful than anyone else's. Such a bond is so powerful because it was fought for; palms have been callused together, the couple emerges from the trenches together and strength has been born.

Without growth, one half gets stuck in the past while the other is darting headfirst into the future. The whole is reaching in opposing directions, disturbing the aim of the unit. My father always told me, "The relationship ends when someone stops growing." Everyone evolves at a different pace, and moving with someone who is going the same pace you are optimizes the efficiency of your stride. The relationship has more room to accelerate when you two are synchronized.

Growing is an infinite experience. Still, a healthy relationship has balance within this infinity. A therapist I once had reminded me that play is just as important as work. Maybe counterintuitively, the phrase, "Work before play" is incompatible with love. If all you two ever do is talk about problems and what needs to change, your relationship will never be enjoyable. You will never be satisfied because *something* will always need to be changed. There must also be time to enjoy one another and the bond you share. Patterns create realities: if the only conversations you have center around problems, then likely all you two have is problems. Inversely, if you only have fun, you're both missing countless opportunities for connection with one another.

With all this in mind, we all make mistakes. No artist is immediately a virtuoso, no ruler is immediately wise, no philosopher is immediately critical; in the same way no partner is immediately decisive. All skills, including growth, empathy, and communication, are learned, not inherent. As teenagers we're all figuring out how to be partners for the first time. For many, it is our first experience of responsibility outside of ourselves. Do not feel obligated to dismiss your standards but be gentle with your expectations on your partner, who is also young and inexperienced. Your partner will frustrate you, you will frustrate them; even so they're doing their best, just like you are.

Forgiveness is how you two keep loving one another. Of course, be mindful of what you are forgiving. If someone is constantly feeding you lies, maybe they really don't deserve to be cultivating a true relationship with you. Contrarily, if your partner forgets a single date, but by and large had been extremely vigilant about them for your whole relationship prior, maybe consider letting that slide. It is up to you to choose what is worth forgiving and what is undeserving of your time. If you have a partner who is critical and unforgiving, it can feel like you're walking on eggshells. But when there's a practice of fair forgiveness, both of you can relax into the relationship and be yourselves. And there's no better feeling than being loved just as you are. Forgiveness is not only an outwardly experience: you forgive your partner but you must also learn to forgive yourself. Even further, being able to apologize is just as important as being able to forgive. "Sorry" needs to be a comfortable word for you both.

There are some things that you should always be able to know in a relationship. It should be undeniable that you can trust your partner. You should know that you don't have to hide any part of yourself from them and perhaps most importantly, you should know that you are safe—not only physically but that your most vulnerable, authentic self is safe with your partner. When you are focusing on empathy, communication, and forgiveness, you'll cultivate a relationship centered on trust in which you both feel safe to grow and evolve.

CHAPTER 2: KNOWING YOURSELF

When you're a teenager, romantic relationships are entirely unfamiliar. In these earliest experiences, we fall headfirst into the lover's world. It is intoxicating in the sense that as we fall so deeply into our partner, we may forget who we are without them. I am often a girlfriend, but I am also a writer, artist, and activist. I am a daughter, sister, niece, granddaughter, a student, and a friend. However, when I become a girlfriend, those other titles can too easily slip my mind, and I've been met with the consequences. By getting engulfed in the world of the lover I have lost close friends and forgotten the passions outside of my relationship that made me who I was in the first place. Somehow, I became the person someone chose to be their girlfriend, but along the way, I lost the defining qualities of myself. All that remained was the title itself.

Before and during a relationship, it is valuable to take the time to explore who you are and realize your own qualities, good and bad. Rather than jumping into romantic relationships, first turn your focus to yourself. Knowing who you are isn't just about being self-aware, it is about understanding your individual identity. Taking time to do this may feel like it's stalling you, but in truth it's supplying you with more stability than anyone else could offer you—stability that will help you not only in attracting a better partner, but also in being one yourself. Learn who you are and what you like to do. If all you think you have is someone else, you will always feel incomplete alone.

So who are you? The answer to that will always be changing, but the best way to discover who you are at your core is to spend time with yourself in pursuit of your own individual happiness. Do what you love to do, just you with you. Carve out time with yourself to enjoy life. If you're not sure yet what your passions are, a good place to start is remembering what you loved to do as a child. Did you spend hours drawing, playing outside, singing, reading, dancing? When's the last experience you had where you were so engrossed in something that the hours seemed to fly by? Find what you love and if you end up in a relationship, commit to continuing to make time for it. People fall in love with *you*, so preserve who *you* are.

If you're feeling incomplete and unfulfilled on your own, invest in something bigger than yourself. Gain a community where you are functionally both dependent and being depended on. Be part of a soccer team, join a club, start writing for the yearbook, or get a local job. It doesn't matter what you do as long as you're not alone in it. Find something that you really, truly need and that simply makes you smile. Apart from your own benefit, imagine this from a partner's perspective. It creates a lot of pressure to have someone solely dependent on you, pressure that incites anxiety. Just like you have a life outside of them, they have a life outside of you as well. If your partner feels like they must be there to stabilize you at all times, they may begin to give up other cherished parts of their lives—a loss which may take down the healthy pillars of your relationship with it. That is not to say you must isolate yourself to firm independence (this in and of itself contradicts being in a relationship), but always find a way to balance your life and theirs.

Being aware of who you are outside of the confines of your relationship makes it easier to be in one and maintain your own standards. When we recognize value in ourselves, we don't need someone else to see it for us. If we are blind to it, we become desperate for someone to assert our relevance. Such desperation is the suffocator of a bond.

Relationships are wonderful but they don't grant you completion of self. You are, by a matter of fact, as valuable alone as you are when joined with another person. Movies and the media in general make us believe that we're not complete until we find our other half. But actually the purpose of love and marriage is not to find the missing piece, but to make our lives richer, more meaningful, and more enjoyable. Nonetheless, especially in our beginning romantic relationships, when someone becomes such a large focus of your attention, your dreams, sports, goals, and academic life can feel irrelevant. All of your passion and energy can get rerouted and dialed into this one person. Knowing who you are and what fulfills you keeps you from becoming unproductive in your *passions*. That is why it's so important to stick with them: your passions make you who you are, not your partner. When you know who you are you can carry yourself taller; you know what is worthy of your time and what love you deserve to have.

No matter how much you know yourself, jealousy is something that often comes up in relationships. It has become blasphemous to discuss jealousy in relationships, but the subject does not need to be taboo. Nearly everyone experiences jealousy, teenagers in particular. Knowing yourself prior to a relationship serves the same purpose as addressing feelings of insecurity. Maintaining that security in yourself makes it harder for you to even begin worrying if your partner wants someone else, since you are clearly enough and they're with you for a reason. Knowing who you are is a freedom that you give yourself. If you are feeling suspicious that your partner has strayed from your relationship, you will be secure enough to understand they may not be a necessity in your life.

When you get used to someone it begins to feel impossible

to live without them or do things separately. You feel lost without them. This is the necessary seventh heaven of being in love; the infatuation is what inspires you to keep reaching for more. The downside to this is that heaven is atemporal. The true world does not stop for the lovers' world. This becomes especially apparent when you don't feel like you have a purpose outside of being a partner. Relying on your partner's affections is simple and secure, but where does that leave you when they're not around?

If you find yourself asking your partner for an excessive amount of reassurance or have a hard time letting them be apart from you, remind yourself that you are okay on your own. Don't forget to compliment yourself. In your moments of individual accomplishment, be your own greatest supporter. Know your own value. When you feel good about yourself, be the first person to acknowledge that. This doesn't mean you can't receive support and compliments from your partner, but know the difference between support and validation. Not only will reaffirming yourself first make you feel more confident, but it will teach your partner how to treat you too. If you show your partner that you know your worth, they won't treat you any less than that. And if they do, you'll know they don't see you for everything you are.

No matter how fulfilling your relationship may feel, do not stop cultivating your external bonds. A richly tended world of your own is significant to keeping your own security. If disagreements ever come up in your relationship, or if something falls through, having a village behind you is invaluable. Your friends are the people that are going to catch your fall. Romantic relationships between teenagers are, for the most part, temporary, ever-changing, but some friendships can last your entire life. Don't forget about them. Not nurturing the rest of your life can leave you in a desert if the relationship ends.

Beyond refusing distinctly bad treatment from a partner —such as verbal or physical abuse, manipulation, infidelity, etc.

—knowing your worth helps you maintain your core values in love. Have you always wanted a partner who's affectionate, who supports you as an equal, makes you laugh, gets along wonderfully with your friends and family? These core values should be your non-negotiables within the relationship. And while everyone has something they are not willing to compromise on, when our feelings take control, it is so easy to let go of our own values. Not just because we want to make sacrifices for a relationship, but because we let our partner's values overshadow our own. While this may feel sufficient in the moment, you'll gradually notice your dissatisfaction returning as you reconnect with yourself. We can only put our true wants aside for so long before they return back to us.

The coexistence of love and values and being able to express them to a new partner will help you find a relationship that is long-living. You may feel strongly about someone, but if they like to smoke and that is against your values in life, this will probably start to be frustrating for you. If you've always been extremely involved with your family, but your partner— who may be wonderful in other countless ways—isn't interested in spending that quality time with your family as well, this will probably become an issue sooner or later. Having contradicting viewpoints doesn't definitively mean either of you are bad or wrong—nor does it mean you're incompatible—it just means you just see things differently. Opposing values may not necessarily cause a relationship to fail, yet it might make you less conducive to dating one another in this stage of your life. A common outlook has the ability to bring two people together, just as sharing an unfamiliar one can. Your core values, your communication style, your likes and dislikes, all stem in large from your upbringing and environment—and it's the same for your partner. As we were all raised in different homes, with different families, it makes sense that we see things differently. You do not need to feel guilty for having desires and opinions of your own, and it should be the same for your partner. It's okay to disagree, and taking the time to cultivate self-awareness and self-confidence will lessen the anxiety of standing up for yourself in your relationship, and help you to set healthy boundaries when necessary.

Outside of physical activities and shared interests, many couples initially struggle with having different communication styles in a relationship. Having a clear grasp of what yours are—before you begin to adapt to someone else's—allows a space to be created where you both deeply understand one another.

One of the ways you can begin to better understand your communication style is to identify your "love language." Many of us have taken love language quizzes online and compared them with our friends and partners for fun, but it can actually become an applicable tool. Your love language is, simply put, the way you prefer to give and receive love. There are five of them: physical touch, words of affirmation, receiving gifts, quality time, and acts of service. Before a relationship, notice how these come up in your life with your non-romantic bonds. Consider, for example, if it means more to you if someone gives you a small gift to show that they love you or if you would rather them assist you in a project.

The clashing of love languages can make partners feel unloved because they aren't receiving the right type of care for themselves. Just as much as you need to understand your own, making an effort to learn your partner's shows them you're paying attention to what makes them happy. Figuring out someone else's love language starts with observation and conversation. Notice what brings them the most joy—do they light up when you give them a heartfelt compliment, or does their happiness come through when you spend quality time together? Once you know both your love language and your partner's, the next step is to reflect on how you can use this insight to strengthen your connection. Are you actively showing them love in a way that resonates with them? Have you communicated your own love language so they can understand what you need? And if your love languages differ, how can you bridge that gap to create a more fulfilling relationship?

Understanding and embracing these differences is an opportunity to grow together, not a barrier to connection. If their love language is physical touch, just remember to put your arm over their shoulder when you're together. If gifts make them feel like you're paying attention to what they love and you see something that reminds you of them—like a specific pastry or even something as small as a sticker featuring something from a movie they love—picking that up could make them feel like you're thinking about them. Embracing both of your love languages doesn't need to be a big deal, it's just the small act of keeping it in the back of your mind and noticing the things that would make them feel loved.

Being aware of how you can and cannot show up in a relationship is just as invaluable as recognizing the things your partner is looking for. We all have blind spots. Although it can be difficult to confront your shortcomings, it's nothing to be ashamed of—in fact doing so makes you an even stronger, more reliable partner to have. Ask yourself, "What do I struggle with in relationships?" What situations or behaviors tend to be issues in your current family relationships and friendships? Do you struggle with confrontations, preferring to stay silent even when something is truly bothering you? Or do you have the opposite behavior, picking a fight when you may not need to? Whatever it may be, if you have this self-awareness about your behavioral patterns, your eyes are open wider to their influence on you. Furthermore, being able to talk openly with your partner about them will help you both foster a more collaborative resolution as these behaviors show themselves.

Why one chooses a partner stems dominantly from their family life. A child with an absent father is likely to seek out someone who satisfies that void as they grow older, looking for a partner who offers a feeling of protection and support. Just the same, if a boy grew up without a mother who took close care of him, he'd probably look for a woman who is deeply affectionate and who gives him an opportunity to rely on her for emotional fulfillment. The tricky part is that, much like seeking validation from your partner, seeking a partner who fills a family wound is just as much of a personal trap—even more so since once you fall into it, it is so comfortable that the "I cannot live without them" tenderness starts to cement, consciously or subconsciously. These patterns are more subtle and elusive, and often materialize as unhealthy relationship dynamics in the future. Our family wounds will always play some part in our relationships, but knowing where they come up helps to clarify why you're in the relationship you're in.

Our family plays a huge part in our romantic relationships. We internalize our environment, so most of our values and habits develop from our circumstances with our parents, in both positive and negative lights. Our family is our first relationship and we take what we "learn" from that and apply it to all of our romantic ones. This is where it becomes important to be conscious of yourself and be open to growing. While it's good to reflect on these patterns before a relationship, 90% of them won't come up until you're actually in one. Being familiar with yourself beforehand offers you an advantage in how to make your relationship reach its peak.

With all of this knowledge combined, relationships not only become more enjoyable, but they no longer feel like a necessity in your life. It's easy to forget about yourself in a relationship, but there are things you can keep in mind to help avoid this. Take time to do things that expand upon the rest of your own life. The little things will make a difference. Remember you are just as important to yourself as your partner is to you.

CHAPTER 3: A WORLD OF CONNECTIONS

With all the things we're trying to figure out as teenagers, building a committed, long-term relationship during this formative, exploratory phase of life can be incredibly rewarding. A deep, one-on-one bond has the potential to offer stability, growth, and fulfillment as you navigate the complexities of being a teenager. However, there's no single "right" path to starting to be in relationships. Love is naturally diverse and takes many forms, all of which can be rich and meaningful. When thinking about which type of romantic relationships you'd like to explore—committed relationships, casual hookups, open relationships, friends with benefits, even long-distance relationships—first think about what it is you're looking to bring into your life. Our wants are dynamic and ever-changing. The discovery of our wants and needs is not immediate, rather we learn about them through the unfolding of our relationships. As our goals and values evolve, so do our desires evolve with us. In this moment, aim to bring experiences into your life that are contributing to the image you have of your own trajectory. Remember, our gift is the boundlessness of our minds. Everything about us is tethered to change—as you grow, your relationships will too.

Just as with anything else in this world, relationships have

CHARLEY SKY GARDNER

their own taboos and sensitivities. One particularly touchy area in modern relationships is the influence of hookup culture. The first thing to know: for all intents and purposes, it's not always a bad thing. Temporary intimacy is not necessarily the defacing of connection. Having an intimate experience ushered exclusively by physical urges (as opposed to romantic ones) can create a purely explorative world for you to be introduced to your own body and emotions. It's certainly not for everyone, but if you feel so inclined there is no shame in that decision. However, recognize that there's no guarantee this world will always be a safe one. If you choose to engage in hookups, it's extremely important to be vividly aware of your surroundings, intentions, state of sobriety, the practice of safe sex, and your partner. Listen to your intuition, make sure you feel safe in all ways and if not, it's always okay to simply call it off and leave. Hooking up can mean very different things to different people, and before or during an experience the intentions of everyone involved should be made clear. For you this may be something you want to keep exclusive to one night, but your partner may think you are looking for more with them. If you're not looking for anything serious, verbalize that plain and clear. While there is, again, no shame in wanting to experiment with this type of intimacy, there is a warranted level of transparency and respect that comes with it. You two may just be mixing bodies, not feelings, but that body is no less fragile and deserving of care than if you were in a committed relationship.

Prior to experimenting with any of this, you need to keep in mind that hooking up is entirely different than having an exclusive partner. You're not usually there to share a meaningful conversation and learn more about one another; rather, you have both made a decision to share the physical. If you don't keep in mind the reality of your decisions, and the likely point of view of your partner, the morning after can be a painful disillusionment.

That said, hookups don't necessarily have to be an impersonal, emotionless experience. There can be real chemistry, if only for a night. But again, it's important to honor what your partner is looking for, and not looking for. Even if you felt something real between you two, they may simply be someone who prefers only casual relationships. Them not wanting something more is not a reflection of you, but rather it's merely what they want for their life at this moment.

Alternatively, if you're someone who's grown very comfortable with one-night stands and doesn't plan to pursue anything further, be mindful of who you invite into yourself. When it is clear to you that someone desires more, don't let them be illusioned. Rather than allowing them to hold onto false hope for something you know isn't going to happen, it's better to let them know gently but firmly that you're not looking for an exclusive relationship. Be clear so they can move on and find someone who has the same desires. Even if your intention was purely to share something good, that kind of disappointment can feel heartbreaking. Honesty in these situations is intimidating, but the aftermath of not being honest is not worth any stress you may have pushed off in the beginning.

In the gray area between hookups and exclusive relationships there are open relationships, among them being friends with benefits. Both are equally common and confusing. While open relationships come in many different forms, usually they're similar to having an exclusive partner, with the exception that you may both seek out other partners as well. Friends with benefits have the potential to be the easiest, or the most complicated, type of relationships. In the same nature as open relationships, being friends with benefits is a decision that has to be made with the understanding that you're not the only one for them. If you're considering it, imagine how it would feel to know your friend had been intimate with someone else while mentally you're only committed to them. Is that potential sting worth being able to explore other people yourself? Explore your feelings but do so in a capacity that gives your partner the respect you both deserve to have.

Open relationships between two partners with the same friend group pose their own unique set of challenges, as these circles are often so tightly knit. They leave very little room for secrets or subtleties, and to be in an open relationship with someone in your friend group is to have your eyes wide open. You may see your intimate partner in turn being intimate with other people. As with hookups, you must be respectful about the decisions you and your partner have made. Open relationships need to be clearly established, with both of you communicating your expectations and not trying to cultivate more with someone who clearly has diverging desires.

Don't enter an open relationship already prepared to campaign against their values to sway them to commitment. You cannot change people, and you shouldn't need to change your desires for other people either. People change when they are ready and wanting to. The right person for you will want what you want: don't worry about needing to redesign your own world for the experience of having them in it. Then it is not your world anymore, but a world made for them.

The relationships that have the potential to be the most fulfilling, and the most devastating, are exclusive, committed relationships. In high school, your first exclusive partners are most likely to come from your friend group. The greatest challenge you face when entering into an intimate bond with a friend is that, when evolving from a simple friendship into something more, there is now both a platonic and romantic relationship to take into consideration. Before plunging into a commitment like this, I would urge you to pause and reflect on what it is you want out of this long-term, and what those consequences could be. Consider the impact of losing this relationship. Assume there will be an end to your romantic relationship, and ask yourself honestly if your friendship can survive that. Are you both able to handle the other finding someone else? If you choose to share a connection like this with your best friend, it can prove to be immensely lightening and joyful. You two share an intimacy in the light you see each other in that no one else may be able to, but recognize the significant risk of losing that bond. Is your friendship more important to you than being able to date them?

There was a time where I had a friend who I was completely inseparable from. We did everything together, and being with them meant nothing but laughter and adventure. Over time, we began reaching a point in our friendship where we were debating, consciously together, whether or not that would look like something more. We were so close and starting to think about the new things we wanted to explore as we were getting older, and we had thought maybe together we could find a space to do that. But without really saying it, I think we both individually realized that what we had together wasn't romantic. We were privileged to be so comfortable together, but we didn't need to *be* together, so we stayed friends to maintain just that. We knew it wouldn't go beyond that, and instead we supported each other in our own relationships. We could've gone further, there's no saying it would have ruined our friendship; however, by making that choice they are still someone I am able to call my friend today.

Ultimately, dating someone from your friend group can be messy since it's so intimately connected with the other important people in your life, but it's also mostly unavoidable. In high school the best approach (if you'd like an approach at all, which you may not), is to determine what is and what is not worth losing. The risks of entering into a relationship with someone in your circle are plentiful, but not necessarily inevitable. If you've had a relationship with someone in your circle before you understand the challenges.

In reality, not only do you risk losing a close friend but you risk losing people in your friend group. The paradox in this situation is that deepening this bond may cancel out another. In deepening or losing your bond with your new partner, you may cancel out another friendship, or the friendship you two once had—you will exchange one for the other. So, if the relationship is sustained, the dynamic of the friend group changes. But that doesn't mean you should try to ignore your own feelings or feel like you can't change what is happening. It's up to you to decide what experience is more valuable here. If someone in your group has had feelings for or been with the person you're now pursuing, they could resent you for your decision. Whether or not the fault is yours is often disregarded as irrelevant in the eyes of young lovers. Your platonic friends can also become frustrated with the time and attention you're putting into your new relationship, feeling like it's taking you away from them. Communication is always key. Instead of letting them slip away, talk to them. Love is not finite—assure them your feelings for your new partner in no way diminish your closeness with them as your friend. It's exhilarating being in love, but your friends are also part of the loves of your life and require the same amount of cultivation. Show them this by still making an effort to hang out with only them and do the things you used to do.

If a relationship with a friend doesn't work out, even if the breakup is amicable, the dynamic of your group is bound to change. Whether the split was easy or not, people will take sides and you have to be prepared for that to happen. Furthermore, your friends' opinions might change about you, even if you gave them no good reason to. Be mindful of what you tell you and your partner's shared friends during the relationship. In high school the fabric of information is controlled by a centripetal force. Whatever you say will follow its curved aim and keep winding through the ears of your peers. High school is not a place of secrets but of data—data that is notably not dictated by fact. Any information you share has the potential to take on a life of its own, so take care with what you share and who you share it with. This doesn't mean you need to keep your guard up all the time, just be mindful of who you're trusting with your personal life.

I had a very short romantic relationship with one of my friends and although it was so brief, our group merged apart when we stopped dating. It wasn't an uncomfortable or cold shift, but it happened nonetheless. Thankfully the person who I had been with and I were able to restore the friendship we once had, but it was clear the group had changed. I missed the way it was before anything had happened, but this change wasn't unnatural—it wasn't even entirely about me and my friend. This was some time ago, and I still have a wonderful friend group with people that I can trust and depend on. The change didn't end my social circle, it was just a part of the evolution of how we found ourselves in relation to one another.

As challenging as all high school relationships can be, long-distance relationships at this age can be especially tricky. Undertaking long-distance love is a remarkable testament to a bond. It requires enhancing everything intimate you two share, mentally and emotionally, to make up for the lack of the physical. A relationship like this is dependent on faith and faithfulness. This commitment asks you to embrace discomfort at times; it asks you to be devoted and content without an immediately tangible lover. A relationship like this requires constant communication and understanding. The distance can make you both feel lonely, so it will demand consistency and patience. Being so far from one another leaves you both much more susceptible to misunderstanding. Know that when arguments arise from their end it's usually out of fear. They cannot be around you, there is no strong sense of security that can be granted to them, so all they have is their nearly blind trust in you.

Having committed to a long-distance relationship myself, what came up the most was miscommunication. The only type of contact we had for months on end was our faces through the screen of our phones. Every day was an effort to maintain intimacy—not just sexually but emotionally. To make up for the distance, we committed to virtual dates on the weekends. On Saturday nights we would log onto Zoom and watch a movie together without any other distractions. If I had a lot to do we'd call and quietly do our own things until the work was done. Committing to a window of uninterrupted time together on the phone wasn't always easy, and some days it just wouldn't work out, but calling on principle every day was a practice that kept us connected.

Getting into any long-term, exclusive relationship is a responsibility. Once you commit yourself to a relationship, your considerations must extend beyond your own. You two are, in many ways, now one. Committing to someone comes with the expectation that you can put yourself second if needed. Not everyone is ready for the weight of that commitment and if someone says that to you, understand that it's not exclusively a reflection of your worth but a disparity in readiness.There is no rush for anyone to love a certain way, so we must meet people who are where we are instead.

As you experiment with different types of relationships, stay aware of your own patterns. Take note of what dynamics are failing and what are successful. Feel out what dissatisfies you versus what fulfills you. If it is difficult for you to give undivided attention to one relationship, experiment with something else. If strings of hookups and open relationships are leaving you empty, seek out a closer bond with one person. There's no right answer, no rules, no correct path, only steps forward in one direction or another. What makes us happy in relationships is as unique and individualized as we are ourselves. Just continue exploring, you are bound to find clues as to what that is along the way.

Adolescence is a time of messy, constant exploration. Out of everything we experience now, most things will not stay with us as we evolve. Throughout our years we will shed our layers, whether or not we wish to. In spite of this, love is not something exclusive to adulthood. You can undoubtedly discover someone with whom you share such a valuable bond that you're eager to be devoted to. At the same time, acknowledge the impermanence of high school relationships. Data suggests that only two out of 100 high school relationships last. There is a bittersweet beauty about this: you have so much time to relearn what the definition of love is over and over again, and to experience different types of bonds that are presently unfathomable to you. What love means to you is, like anything else, not an absolute or a definitive. Joy and growth come from continuing to explore love in all its manifestations. You do not have to stifle your love. Embrace everything.

CHAPTER 4: MANIFESTING RELATIONSHIPS

As children, we live largely in the world of our imagination. We play pretend, create elaborate fantasies and adventures, and daydream constantly. But as we enter the period of adolescence, this world must amalgamate with reality. In other terms, our inner world must coalesce with the outer one. We will start to more consciously realize ourselves and what our lives look like in the context of the real world. In this way, we begin to find out who we are. We then have the ability to coherently decide which path suits us through a messy process of trial and error. In the same way, we can discover the person who we will spend our life with.

There is no immediate cheat code to finding a partner, *but* there is a little tool my father taught me that can bring clarity to your search for a romantic partner, and which he used to find the love of his life. It uses the tool we were so adept at using as children: imagination. Manifestation is where imagination comes in here—it is the process of attracting what you want into your life. Similar to goal-setting, you choose an outcome and employ the strength of your own mind to bring that into reality.

The process is relatively simple. When you're ready, find

something to write with and on. Then, think about everything you want in your person. It's difficult to find a good partner when you don't know what that's meant to look like. Put yourself in the position of an author writing a story: there are no boundaries, anything you can possibly imagine you can put onto that paper. You can create any world you dream of. Imagine you're designing a world for yourself in which you feel nothing but peace. Who is there with you? What is their personality like? What are their values? How are they supporting you? What are you two achieving together? Make this person as real as possible, really imagine what it feels like to be with them. That said, don't attach yourself to specific physical details. The looks will come with the right person. Be prudent. You ought to be meticulous about what you write in this, making it vexingly specific.

An example:
1. Age ranged between 16 and 17
2. Provides consistent positive affirmation, without me needing to ask for it
3. Enjoys PDA
4. Appreciates and is curious about the arts
5. Has a supportive family, who I can be close with
6. Supportive of my life goals
7. Never directs harsh words at me or curses
8. Doesn't get unhealthily jealous
9. Stable emotionally with themselves as well as me
10. Hygiene aware
11. Likes to be in the outdoors
12. Is an athlete like me and understands my schedule

For context, my list had about 75 qualifications and my father's had about 150. A few of the things I had written down were: uses positive affirmation without me having to ask; doesn't rely on me to plan all of our outings; puts in effort to make me a part of their family; dependable and can hold me accountable. As you try to find the right person for you, you may find some of the things on your list become less important, or others indispensable. Luckily, the list is not cemented—you may change it as frequently as you would like. In the midst of all of the heat and excitement of dating you have to realize how much of this is truly within your own control. Every relationship we have we choose to be in for one reason or another, which means you can choose to have the one you really want.

Having this list doesn't mean you are inordinately reading it over and over. Just write it and let it be. Simply by creating it, your subconscious mind will know what to be looking for and it will point you in that direction. I wrote my list just one month before entering what would become, at that time, my longest relationship and first love (by my own standards). Amazingly, roughly 70 out of the 75 things I jotted down matched perfectly with that partner. Although the relationship eventually ended (and since then some of the things on my list have changed or been completely let go), that relationship was the perfect one for me to experience at the time.

I know that the process may seem trivial at first glance, and I couldn't argue with that skepticism. It does sound too easy that you could merely think about what you want and then it will happen. At first I thought my father was hilarious for doing this, but, even if just indirectly, it worked. Our power over our own lives reaches much farther than we know. And if nothing else, what do you have to lose?

Whether we realize it or not, we are actually manifesting all of our relationships. Our thoughts have power, and our inner world undoubtedly bleeds into our outer one. What we think, feel, imagine, and believe ripples into our reality. Our beliefs around relationships—whether they're mimics of the dynamics of our parents, toxic patterns, or things we've internalized from the media—invite in the type of relationships we "want." Creating a list of positive attributes can help guide better people into our lives and change what our subconscious is already finding for us.

When you write this list, do it with a purpose. Clear out

time to write and really think about exactly what you want. If you write the list on a whim, you won't invest your mind into it. Once you do it thoughtfully and thoroughly, notice when the people in your life and the words on the page begin to resemble one another. If someone comes into your life who starts to feel more and more familiar, pursue them. Give it time as well. I found my partner relatively soon after, but that's not always the case. Keep trusting that the person you're supposed to be with during this period of your life is out there. And above all, know that you deserve to be with that person.

CHAPTER 5:
PRESSURES AND
EXPECTATIONS

At one point or another, we've all wanted something more from someone in our lives. When we love someone our expectations rise with how much they mean to us. Perhaps we wished they would have been more helpful about something or we hoped they'd carve out more time to spend with us. You've probably felt the same pressure to do or be something more for them too. Especially in our current fast-paced society, pressure is a constant. At any given time, we have about six different pressures bearing down upon us—from ourselves, our families, our partners, society, our peers, and social media. There seems to be an impossible fight for perfecting something just a little, or a lot, out of reach. Recognizing what is constricting us is the first step to alleviating the pressure.

One of the biggest sources of constriction—no matter your gender, age, race, etc.—is society, and the roles we're expected to play in it. Since the beginning of civilization, both men and women have been given gender roles to fulfill. Men have been expected to provide for and take care of women, and, more often than not, to disregard their own emotions to fulfill that expectation. Women are expected to carry all of the emotional weight of the relationship and to be submissive, and in some cases, more of an accessory than a partner. Even if we're not being told outright to uphold them, traditional gender roles are reinforced everywhere we look—from TV shows to magazines to movies to every form of marketing. Every female knows the pressure to be pretty, to temper her anger in order to be well-liked, to put her needs second to play the role of the compassionate caregiver. And every male can understand the fear of being seen as weak unless he's physically strong and emotionally assertive, or of being seen as a failure if lacking a successful and lucrative position.

Although these strict gender roles are becoming more abstracted every day, they have been ingrained in us for so long that we still feel the pressure of them. Whether or not we realize it, we often enforce them onto our partner as well. It's not our fault for expecting these standards from a relationship—they've been the status quo for hundreds of years. However, it is surely our responsibility to identify them and actively broaden our frame of mind.

There are a lot of societal barriers to break in our relationships. For one, it shouldn't be assumed that the male partner will be the sole financial provider in the relationship, just because they are a man. Now, some guys are happy to play the role of provider and if that's what fulfills both partners, then that's what works for them. At the same time, it's quite reasonable for your male partner to expect you to pay for a meal every now and then. A balance can be set by simply splitting the cost of things 50-50. For girls with male partners, recognize the pressure they may feel always having to be the financial supporter in the relationship. As with anything, this is something that can be easily communicated. Making an effort to discuss who's paying for what before it becomes an issue can save you both some unnecessary conflict. There are countless ways to approach the balance (and disruption) of traditional gender roles, and this approach for every relationship will be as unique as the individuals within it. Every culture and household has different approaches to gender roles, so make an effort to discuss it with your partner.

Regardless of your philosophies or roles, providing for your partner should always be done out of love, not obligation. If the provider holds their contribution over their partner's head, it is no longer a kindness but a means of control. Of course, it is valid for the partner spending their hard-earned money on the relationship to expect recognition for what they do, and they can rightfully acknowledge their contributions to the relationship. However, if there is a situation, such as an argument, where the provider says something to the extent of, "Well I buy so much for you so...", their contributions are no longer selfless. There is a line between self-advocacy and manipulation. Providing for someone you love, emotionally or financially, should never be an intentional way of establishing a power imbalance between two individuals. It should be a product of your dedication to one another.

One thing any woman will understand is the expectation to be agreeable—to be easy-going and non-argumentative. Even though it may seem over-dramatized in the media, which has no doubt led to the controversy surrounding the idea of overly aggressive and man-hating feminism, this expectation for women to be pleasant and consenting still plays a role in the large context of our social groups. As females in society, we often live under the shadow of the labels "emotional," "bitchy," "dramatic," as well as many other creative terms. I'll unveil an incredible secret: *everyone* gets bitchy and emotional. Perplexingly, these titles are not in fact exclusive to the female sex. In an effort to avoid such stereotypes, girls often try to impersonate something unfeeling. A message to my fellow women: your emotions do not make you burdensome or ridiculous. Feeling does not make you too much for the world and your emotional process does not need to look beautiful. It is okay to set boundaries and not be understanding of something or someone that is smothering you. And to the men, you are not exempt from being emotional either. Pause before putting down your girlfriend for expressing what she feels. And just as you should let her be angry and assertive, she should let you be scared, or uncertain, or vulnerable.

If your partner lets him- or herself feel safe enough to open up to you, create a space for them to do that. Vulnerability is like revealing an open wound to someone. If someone shows that to you, you then hold the responsibility to not infect that wound. Your job isn't to *mend* the wound, but to acknowledge it and be there with it. Oftentimes all anyone needs to start healing is for someone to listen to them with attention and non-judgment. Vulnerability is a risk and we all need one another's support in getting comfortable with it.

For most of us, we've always had social media in our lives. It has become a source of community for our generation, especially after we needed to rely on it so much during COVID-19. As important as it is to our generation though, social media has begun to place unhealthy expectations on everyone in society, and in relationships, specifically men. The phrase, "If they wanted to they would" has morphed into a harmful conjecture that can impulsively demean someone's actions before they even take place. In popular media we often see guys walking through snowstorms and putting on huge, expensive displays of affection for their girlfriends. While this is incredibly romantic and exceptional, this image can project inferiority on already hard-working partners. In truth, some guys don't show their love with huge displays of romance, and many of them may be exerting themselves much more than you know for your happiness. For some, being consistent in saying a simple, "I love you" every morning may be the ultimate show of affection, or bringing you your favorite coffee before a long day. I was with someone who made a point to always get takeout with me after I had a big race. To your male partner, doing something that may appear small could be exactly what they think is the right thing for you, and that dedication to consistency can be more meaningful than anything else.

Of course, there are always instances in which people really aren't trying that hard—and that's a separate conversation you can have—but don't discredit what your partner does for you. Chances are, they are trying their best. If you feel especially dissatisfied with how your partner is showing their affection and truly feel like you need the bigger gestures, there are a few things you can do. For one, you can compromise and make an effort to appreciate your partner in the smaller ways they express their love for you. Another thing is to communicate your dissatisfaction to them and give them a chance to make a change. Or, you can decide that it's important enough to you to find someone who values grand displays as much as you do. You deserve nothing less than what makes you happy, just as much as a hard working-partner also deserves your gratitude.

As well as the society we grow up in, our immediate environment of friends and family plays an equally significant role in our relationships. The relationships we're most exposed to as children, usually that of our parents', has an inescapable influence on how we approach relationships as young people. If someone has grown up with parents who compliment each other frequently, they'll want that verbal affection in their lives. If another person has parents who fight regularly, having a partner who's argumentative and aggressive may seem, to them, like the norm, or any conflict could bring them back to that unpleasant piece of their childhood. How our families actually *feel* about our partners can influence our relationships, too. Someone with a close relationship to their parents may be reluctant to date someone they disapprove of, while another may enjoy rebelling against their parents' wishes.

At this point in our lives, equally and likely even more important in shaping our relationships is the opinions of our friends. Peer pressure deeply impacts how we act with our partners. In pursuit of belonging, we seek the approval of our peers. For our friends to disapprove of our relationship would cause us to reevaluate it ourselves; inversely having a coveted relationship can persuade us to pursue it further, regardless of whether or not it's truly beneficial to our own well-being.

Many of our dating habits mirror what we see around us. If our friends are partial to hooking up, our decisions are impacted even before they are made. Seeing the majority of the people you care about and respect beginning to explore physical intimacy will have an influence on when you decide you're ready. Similarly, watching your friends treat their partners a certain way will impact your understanding of dating. It is inevitable that your friends form opinions about your relationships too. Sometimes, those opinions can be biased based on their own personal experiences, but they may also provide insight into things we are blind to in our relationships. In love we are immediately somewhat blindsided, this is fairly an essential beauty to the experience. Our naivety, the novelty of the experience, the departure from perfect reason and rationality lights the fire. We're not meant to be rational in the first blows of love, and especially at this age, we are deeply impressionable individuals, and who we surround ourselves with will impact how we conduct ourselves. While they're not the only factor, our friends certainly play a role in whether we think it's the norm to conduct ourselves in relationships with grace and understanding, or with reactivity and drama. The right friends may be guides for relationships, but don't rely on them or what you see in them. If your friends have harmful relationships with others, consider what it is you actually want before imitating it. Your choices are yours and yours alone.

In relationships, people show up based on what they think is expected of them. But everyone has different needs, and every partner expects different things in their relationship—particularly regarding how often you two are in contact. Texting is one of the most preferred forms of communication for our generation, but the trouble with texting is that everything about it is open to interpretation. The fragility of texting stems from its permissive nature. Lacking any vocal and visual cues, a single sentence can be interpreted a hundred different ways. Even the time it takes someone to reply, or not, can put us into a tailspin without knowing what the person we texted is actually doing at that moment. Everyone has their own texting style and pace. Sometimes one person sends more texts than the other, which can make them feel like they're doing all the work to keep the conversation going. On top of that, we each have our own "texting dialect." A simple "K" might feel dismissive to one person, even if it's meant as warmly as someone else's, "Okay, that sounds great."

I hear complaints about texting all the time, especially when it comes to things like the difference between an, "I love you" and a quick, "ily." I've had friends come to me convinced their partner doesn't care about them simply because of a certain texting style. To be fair, a shift in tone can be a valid concern, especially if you know your partner really well—but it doesn't always mean something's wrong. The best way to navigate the uncertainty is to ask questions directly. In this case, don't always just trust your gut; our reactions often come from our own perspective, not theirs. If you're really worried, skip the guessing game and the round of asking friends for interpretations. Just talk with your partner. Remember, your friends' interpretations, like yours, come with their own biases and may not be accurate at all.

As relationships get going, you two will have to figure out what your preferences are in every aspect of your relationship—which involves exploring many questions like, "How much can I touch my partner in public?" Everyone's answer to this is different. Some are ready to embrace this level of connection, while others may need a while to acclimate before taking the next step. The amount of intimacy that our partners are comfortable showing to the public will vary. (The level of intimacy you're both comfortable with in private is a bigger discussion, which I've devoted all of Chapter 10 to).

I was with someone that will, for this purpose, go by Theodore, who had much more conservative views on PDA than I did. I wanted his arms wrapped around me any chance we could get, and I was completely unbothered being close to him in front of other people. He was very proud to be with me, and very open about our relationship, but felt like physical affection should be something that we just had for ourselves and didn't need to show off to the public eye. Needless to say, I didn't appreciate the modesty. However, neither of our perspectives were invalid. Theodore had grown up with parents that were rather traditional, who felt intimacy was a private matter to just be shared behind closed doors. My observations growing up had been that the fluidity of touch was the standard, if not the expectation. As with any form of intimacy, any level of PDA shouldn't be expected from your partner, nor should it be done out of obligation. It is a conversation to be had to ensure all members of a relationship are comfortable.

As much external pressure as we feel from society and our family and friends, no one puts more pressure on ourselves than us. Whenever you feel like you're falling short of any of these expectations, remember that we cannot know how to get relationships right the first time, or the second time, or the third time. In fact, we will never just *know*, because we and everyone else around us are constantly changing. In fact, remove the word "perfect" from your vocabulary entirely. There is no such thing as the perfect partner. Strive to be better, don't strive to be perfect. Now more than ever, we will make mistakes. Our judgment is relatively uninformed so we will mess up, and that is, indeed, completely fine. As a matter of fact, it is better than fine: if you mess up it means you're attempting something unfamiliar. You are trying to be better, and all we can do in a relationship is try, revise, and improve.

That said, unvoiced expectations morph into silent pressures. The two become deadlocked by one person's hurt and the other's misunderstanding. Now one person is begging the question, "What do you want from me?", and a particle of dissatisfaction has gradually expanded into a glooming cloud. Unfortunately no one can read your mind—all they have is the information you give to them. It doesn't help anyone if you sit in your anger expecting them to decipher what the problem is: that's a choice you are making. Even if the latter is intimidating, talk with them, understand one another.

CHAPTER 6:
MANIPULATION
AND CONTROL

Manipulative relationships are perhaps the most difficult ones to break out of. Manipulative partners tend to be extremely emotionally intelligent, and therefore very charming. At the beginning, they may immerse you in love and praise, knowing just what you want to hear. As the relationship progresses however, their need to control slinks in. The pain of this figure usually comes from having had a deeply self-explored practice of pain. Manipulative partners often feel out of control in their own lives, whether this is from their own family dynamics, issues at home or school, or some past personal trauma.

In this type of relationship, there is a constant push and pull that keeps you engaged and infatuated with the pain. Manipulative partners make you think you need to be in pain or distort your definition of pain into pleasure. It becomes comfortable to be in the discomfort—it begins to feel like a necessary experience. They understand your nervous system. Partners like this can feel out threads that tie you together, even if sometimes unintentionally, and with a gentle tug, they might make one unravel, drawing you to be more dependent on them. Often, they themselves begin to feel like the threads that tie you together. Relationships like this are all-consuming. You lose sense of the reality of your situation. Your partner's reactions to even the smallest things are so extreme you stop knowing what's real, and at some point you get so tired of trying to understand whose fault it is that you end up simply accepting it. To break out of this, you must remember something about love: it is not meant to be easy, but is not meant to be frightening either.

Manipulative relationships parallel addiction. You need it but to have it is to bring harm to yourself. Literally you do not need it; regardless, your life has now been redefined with this desire. Life without it now seems less. Manipulation—unnerving, addictive push and pull—can disguise itself as exceptional love. Manipulation may wear the mask of charming gestures or expensive gifts. It is, however, only concealing a greater reach for control. Manipulative partners may purport themselves as romantics, but their objective is to secure themselves. Everything must be able to be held in their palms.

Control externalizes insecurity. Manipulative partners try to find a way to make you depend on them *because* they don't feel dependable. This may come from the environment around them being chaotic and unstable, or from an internal sense of unworthiness and self-doubt. They may tell you they "need you," or that they "can't survive without you." Or they may spin it the complete opposite way, telling you, "You need me." After a while of hearing this your subconscious adopts it as fact. Not to belittle life to the physical act of living itself, but in point of fact, you *can* feel, breathe, taste, smell, and see without the other; your heart beating is not reliant on your coexistence, although it may completely and entirely feel like it. No romantic relationship needs a martyr or a savior—it produces a dynamic of unhealthy dependency for validation. When you have to adopt one of these roles you've become trapped within them. If you are constantly expending all your energy on acting as a savior for your partner, rescuing them from crisis after crisis of their own making, you'll have no energy left for your own life. When you constantly fight and then make up, or need to talk them off a ledge, or prove your devotion time and again, it can feel purposeful at first but ultimately it drains your resources.

One of the most blatant indicators of manipulation is the silent treatment. You're left alone in your own head wandering in circles of unfounded guilt, so you become desperate for them to tell you what's wrong. You begin to see them as the answer to your problem, rather than the cause of it, and suddenly you feel entirely at fault. You'll find yourself apologizing for nearly everything in the end. Often, you won't even know what you're apologizing for, but it will feel right to do so. You'll feel like you should be apologizing more, then you feel so guilty you will keep catering to them. "I need to solve the problem, I need to fix it, I can fix it. I can make everything okay. I can help them." Or, you will know it's wrong but, as noted earlier, you'll be too depleted to stand up for yourself anymore, and in that resignation you will let them maintain control over the relationship. You will shove aside your gut instincts, and focus only on the feelings that ensure your relationship—as nothing else will feel so right or important.

After the adrenaline and excitement of the relationship settles, your partner's unhealthy (and often, very conveniently timed) neediness will slowly come up in small parts of your life. When you're out with friends they'll need you to be on alert for them contacting you, so you begin to feel afraid to not have your phone on hand. Of course, it is entirely reasonable to expect your partner to check in once or twice to ensure their safety and to know they're being thought of. If it is done out of fear or jealousy though, the intention warps the legitimacy of their requests. Your partner should feel secure enough to be alone and not always around you. Unless that's something you both want, it can be demanding for both partners. On the other hand, when their control is feeling unstable, they may withdraw their affection completely. They may stop responding to your texts or answering your calls, in the hopes of regaining the upper hand by you begging them to reply. Again, this accomplishes nothing real except putting unnecessary strain on both of you. If they see something on social media that you liked or that someone followed you, they shouldn't immediately be accustory of you; they shouldn't yell at you or ghost you over something unfounded. It's not your responsibility to regulate their emotions, it's theirs. That doesn't mean, however, that they cannot expect anything of you to feel emotionally secure. Healthy dependency is essential, but it shouldn't always rest on the shoulders of one person.

Manipulative partners know exactly what to say to reach you. They've mastered your blind spots. The pull they've created gives itself away in slight changes in their faces or intonations. Their word choice will be intentional in trying to provoke a feeling from you. In order to make you start to question yourself, they create and define an acute distinction of what's good behavior and bad behavior on your end of the relationship. You may hear, "You would do it if you actually loved me," "How many times do I have to apologize?", or something as simple as, "Oh, okay I guess." Often we feel anxiety in our first relationships, but most comments like this are not particularly incidental.

Oftentimes in films and books, we see lovers demanding their partner make some big show to prove their love. Romeo ignores his family feud with Juliet for her love; Rose and Jack try to be together even with the burning segregation of their classes. It's a romantic request to have someone show how much they care about you, but not always a healthy one. When you're constantly being asked to "prove" your love, you feel guilty all the time. Now you *must* be better, regardless of likely already being stressed from trying so hard—there must be something you're doing wrong. As long as you feel unworthy, you are reliant on them for validation. You've lost your control. They now define good and bad, enough or not enough. To be fair, this is not exclusively a manipulative move and may stem from personal insecurity on their part. But there is still an important difference between asking someone for healthy shows of love, and making someone fight for their approval of love. Romance is an invaluable and wonderful part of being in love with someone; a partner constantly being questioned about their feelings is not.

Fireworks are immediately breathtaking. You are captivated in a few seconds of organized color. Then it's gone, perpetually irrelevant. Nothing has changed after the instant excitement of the whole phenomenon fades away. "Love bombing" is the same: fleetingly, profusely comforting. Sporadic displays of extreme affection keep everything else excusable, so you cannot stand up for yourself without being called unappreciative. Your partner would do everything in their control to redirect any faults onto you. And even if they do acknowledge their faults, it's likely they will not truly change their actions. You'll feel temporary satisfaction in their newly cultivated character and begin to forgive everything, then it will revert back, quietly but surely. A person seeking control won't truly change, they will just appear to work on things. Manipulative people are often living with such insecurity that their inner world is deeply uncomfortable, and seeking outward control is the only way they know how to attempt to manage it. Not to say people can't ever change, but the truth is, they will only ever choose to change on their own. It's not something you can choose for them. It needs to be their decision, when they're ready, and in their own time.

Humans are, more than anything, not one dimensional beings. No one man or woman is evil or pure. We are composed of imagination and story, our actions project off of our feelings. Manipulation is thus not definitively malicious or even conscious. When people are in a deep enough place of pain they might become oblivious to themselves. When a manipulative person easily reacts defensively, they may feel genuinely hurt, unfortunately making it even harder to reach them. The only way to dictate whether or not a relationship with these patterns can evolve is by setting boundaries. If you think your partner is overstepping, vocalize it to them. If you can, think about what you're going to say beforehand to ensure you truly get your point across to them, rather than reacting solely on emotion in the moment. Expect that they will immediately get defensive, attacking everything you're saying and making you feel ridiculous for even bringing it up. Even if you've just made a very small request, you'll probably start to feel guilty for even expressing your feelings in the first place. Guilt is one of human kind's most valuable emotions—it is a reflection of our evolution to conscious, empathic beings—but it shouldn't be the defining emotion in your relationship. Your partner may try to turn things around to be your fault, but only just enough that you still feel like they're not the one unjustly placing all the blame on you. It's important to stay true to what you are feeling and remind yourself that what you're asking for is okay. Even though the way they're reacting is because they're afraid of something, you still deserve to be heard. The relationship is not theirs, it is both of yours.

A request may turn into an argument or guilt trip and from then on you'll be too afraid to give any more input. You'll notice them using nice things they've done for you in the past as justification for an issue, even if absolutely unrelated (the fireworks). In most cases you may get gas-lit out of your dilemma and somehow you will end up returning the apology to them. This pattern is hard to break: as soon as you try to remove yourself they will do everything they can to keep you. You will feel like you're the one at fault, because that's what your relationship has trained you to feel like. Then you'll need to ask yourself, is this love?

You lose yourself in a manipulative relationship. You become molded to an image of what your partner is trying to create. If you stop recognizing yourself, commit to finding who you are again. Remove yourself from the intensity of the relationship. Try spending a whole day with friends, or do something by yourself that you love for a few hours without your phone nearby. This can let you *feel* as to whether the relationship is truly making you happy. From the outside, watch the movement of the environment you've been in. Is stepping out of it a relief? Do you feel like you can finally relax and enjoy yourself again? If so, reach out to somebody. Receiving an outside perspective allows you to see your relationship more clearly here, and in some cases, helps you see if you're enabling your partner's actions.

Partnerships should help you grow and discover new aspects of yourself. Being in love should expand your world, not pull you into a smaller one. In a manipulative relationship you become someone else, someone who exists to satisfy another's image. Now, your only goal is keeping them from going off the rails or getting upset. A relationship cannot be built by fear, it will consume itself.

Bottom line, your partner will put themselves in a place of being the one who is wronged and, because you care about them, you'll want to console them. Leaving them will feel like leaving home, but home is not always safe. When going through this process you will feel conflicted. What if it was really all your fault? What if you do need them? What if you're losing the person you're supposed to be with? Let go of these thoughts. If they were right for you, you wouldn't have to be considering leaving. Let go for yourself, trust, even if blindly, that everything will be okay without them. You will be okay.

CHAPTER 7: STAGES OF A RELATIONSHIP

Y ou're looking at each other from across the room, you can feel your heart in your chest. They're looking at you and your mind is rapidly trying to figure out if that look in their eyes is meant only for you. You know you want to talk to them, but you're scared. You search every corner of your mind trying to find the most golden thing to say to them, but then, they're gone. Dammit. How are you supposed to compose yourself enough to talk to them? What if they didn't mean to look at you that way, or you made the whole thing up in your head?

You could spend a lifetime caught up in your own thoughts trying to answer these questions, but you'll find that you're perpetually too late—the moment will have passed before you can do anything about it. The only way you'll ever truly know if someone's interested in you is to talk to them. Overthinking is the greatest thief of time. If you've been in relationships before, think about how they came to be. Likely, by one of you two being brave enough to initiate that first conversation. Rejection is terrifying, you are taking a risk. And to be blunt, you will get rejected eventually—it's an inevitable part of the dating world. Sometimes the people we think we want aren't actually supposed to be with us, as timelessly annoying as that is to say. Regardless, the only thing you have to lose is a missed opportunity. Don't wait for the right moment, there won't be one. Time waits for no man's fear —you have to create the moment. The very person you've been agonizing over talking to may have been waiting for *you* the whole time.

If you happen to be close friends with the person you're interested in, wanting to pursue them romantically can be even more confusing. The line between friendliness and flirtiness is a blurred and distracted one. Still, the idea is the same: be bold and up front with them about your curiosity. Do this yourself, face to face if possible. I would passionately advise against asking someone to play messenger for you, but it's not always the worst idea to get the help of a friend. If you two have a mutual friend, ask them to learn a bit more about your interest's romantic life; ask if they've been interested in anyone or if they're already dating someone. The first interaction of asking someone out leaves a big impression on your partner though; don't ask someone else to facilitate that experience for you.

This first conversation can be awkward, of course. You're both nervous and excited so you both want to leave a good impression, which usually results in saying something rather silly and quite out of character for you. In my experience though, the right person will find it endearing, so don't pay it any mind. Once I was going on a date with someone (which was long overdue), and he had the sides of his hair shaved off, which I'd never really seen before and liked a lot. So I asked him about it and while he was telling me why he did it, without giving it any thought, I reached out and seized the side of his head so I could see it. It took me a second to realize I had grabbed this guy's head who I had just barely met but, after a couple seconds of blank staring at each other, we started laughing and it became a shared joke that we held together for a long time.

As tempting as it may be to say some awe-inspiring, charming lines on a first date, prioritize authenticity. The person sitting across from you wants to know who *you* are. That doesn't mean you shouldn't be charming, that's part of it sure, but stay true to yourself. The most advantageous thing for you to do on a first date is to be intentional about listening. Not only does it make the other person feel heard, but it helps *you* know if you actually want to be with them. First and foremost, make sure you even want them before trying to make sure they gain interest in you.

If it's difficult for you to make conversation on a first date, do something with them. Doing something enjoyable together helps foster genuine bonding and opens up much more about your compatibility. Going to a cafe, arcade, pottery class, aquarium, or even just somewhere to walk around together creates a space for you both to relax. Most people opt for seeing a movie, and while I think movies are a fantastic relaxing, casual date, your ability to get to know one another is overshadowed by the film. In the end though, if it's the right person it won't matter what the date really is, it will just end up working because you two will be making it work together. A bad first date also doesn't mean you don't have any compatibility. When you really like somebody, it can be intimidating and awkward. It doesn't really matter if you stumble a little on the first date. What matters is if there's an effort from both sides to keep seeing each other, because you guys feel there is something there you need to have in your lives.

When you meet someone you feel strongly about, the excitement and adrenaline can make you forget about even having a first date. It's not essential, but slowing down and committing to one sets a really nice foundation for how you get to know each other. My best first date experience was getting dinner at a little restaurant in town. We had walked there together and rather than sitting across from one another, he sat right down next to me. I didn't even need to stop and think about what to say, as if I had been talking to a very old friend. There was a mutual understanding between us, like we had known one another our whole lives and were just finally catching up. Not every experience will be like that; however, in my experience, when it's right it just works. It's effortless.

Once a new relationship begins, it unfolds in several layers, set in motion by the first: "Bliss and Excitement," better known as the honeymoon stage. This initial launch feels like the pinnacle of a lifetime, a time of pure enjoyment and innocent infatuation. Your relationship is new and wondrous, as if you've discovered a little pocket of infinity. Your hands and mind will feel created only for the purpose of knowing them. You will both feel incredibly euphoric and there's a science behind that. When you begin a relationship, your brain is overwhelmed by dopamine and norepinephrine, two neurotransmitters that make you feel as if you're floating. When you're around someone you're attracted to, these chemicals are released in the brain, causing you to feel carefree, blissful, and completely focused on the object of your affection. The honeymoon stage is unavoidable, and it should be. This is an amazing and exciting time to deeply enjoy one another. Cherish this time—there is no need to be hasty and start focusing on what will come next. Hold time as it comes to you, not as you see it coming.

When you're in the honeymoon phase everything about your partner will seem perfect. You are enamored with your new person, every single thing they do will seem immaculate. Any sense of impulsivity will feel justified when you've struck such gold. They are everything now and you want to dive headfirst into all the possibilities of your relationship. The best way to stay grounded during this time is to stay absolutely present in it. You have discovered a new world, but it's still an unfamiliar environment. Fairly, you're so absorbed with desire for this new person that your mind is incapable of slowing down here, so force a healthy layer of caution upon yourself. As connected as you feel to this person, you don't know who they really are yet. Your image of them is distorted by the pure adrenaline and excitement you're feeling. You're just moving away from having a crush, and part of having a crush is having a fondness for an appealing lack of information about the other person. Not to say that's not real, but you've never had to address any issues or grow with this person.

You don't know how they respond to serious situations. One's response to crisis is equally as valuable as their response to love. Enjoy this phase and stay in it, don't use what you're feeling now to jump ahead.

Bittersweet as it may be, the initial honeymoon phase is bound to end. The transition into the second phase, what I like to call, "Learning and Trusting," is both a trying and necessary one. If the relationship remains static in the compelling honeymoon phase, a deeper connection cannot be formed. You are still both only connected to a very specific version of one another. You are in love with the way they smile, how fast they drive you in their car, how they pronounce your name, and the way they laugh at something they find funny. The honeymoon phase does not end or leave, rather it goes through a chromatic metamorphosis. You have fallen in love with the way this person has become your light, now you must understand them with respect to their darkness. As you discover one another's flaws you will shed the layer of innocent euphoria, as is part of the natural evolution of a relationship.

In this process of reciprocal learning, you remember that your partner is not in fact a perfect entity, excluded from the flaws of humanity. The honeymoon high has subsided, and things that once seemed endearing may now feel exasperating. You may love how many ideas and plans they come up with, until you begin to realize they never follow through with any of them. As you come back down to earth, tie yourself back to reality. Connect with friends, spend time with your family, remember your hobbies; reacquaint yourself with who you are. When your brain can no longer be entirely fulfilled by the chemicals being released from being with your partner when the high wears off, maintaining balance in the other aspects of your life supports you both in laying a robust foundation for a stable relationship. It's not to say you are beginning to like them any less, you're just remembering that there are other things going on in your life.

In adjusting to going through life alongside one another, you will be made to slow down and readjust together. These points will serve as way stations during your relationship. In these periods in which things cease to run smoothly, you're bound to experience disagreements or miscommunications, complicated by feelings of apprehension. You two both have different ways you go about your lives and those will certainly not always easily converge. As you work through the things that begin coming up, any differences in your communication styles will quickly become very apparent. For example, maybe you two have been talking on the phone every night for the past month, but now your responsibilities call you back, making your talks more of a chore than the luxury they once were.

It's time to pick your battles. You two are different people; instead of letting those differences pull you apart, view them as an opportunity to progress who you are. Be intentional in discovering one another—becoming fluent in someone else is a beautiful thing if you choose to enjoy it as such. Ask questions, adventure aimlessly. The honeymoon phase never really passes *if* you are with the right person. Keep rediscovering what constitutes your love. Knowledge of another being is just as remarkable as knowing the dynamics of their body. Having the serious conversations can be nerve racking; staying in bliss is comfortable, there's nothing to lose in the pleasure. Still, if you both put them off, the unsaid will corrode your bond. To clarify, by serious conversations I do not intend to tell you to begin your five-year plan. More so I mean, how much time do you want to be spending together, and how will that function in motion with your current goals. Be clear on your expectations. You may be a great match, but your priorities may still pull you in very different directions. If one person wants to focus all their free time on their sport, for example, and you are very extroverted and like going to parties on the weekends, you're going to end up with a lot of disagreements on how you spend your time.

Feeling bored after the end of the honeymoon phase also

shows you your actual wants regarding human connection. If you are left feeling unfulfilled after the high of the first meetings wears off, you should stop and look at your relationship. Does this person have the qualities you truly value and desire, and you simply need to shift something within the existing relationship to feel excited about it again? Or do you need to find something different, whether that be someone better suited for you or a new type of relationship dynamic? If you are on the receiving end of that, do your best to be non-judgmental about your partner's desires and yours as well, even with the frustration—there's no one right or wrong way to approach relationships, especially at this stage in our lives. You shouldn't be with someone who doesn't want what you want anyway. We all deserve the freedom to make our choices, but we also all deserve reciprocation, so hold yourself and others to that standard.

After the exhilaration of meeting and the realization of one anothers flaws, you reach the third phase, "The Crossroads." A good question to ask yourself as you enter this phase is, "Will this relationship improve my life?" Are the issues you two have something you can work on together? No relationship is perfect, but are the imperfections bad enough that this will be more painful than fulfilling? I cannot tell you how to choose, no one can. Deciding to stay with the relationship, rather than leave it, means you are ready to commit to growing and working with your partner to better yourselves and your relationship. You have to decide what will make for a good, healthy relationship. This is where the phrase, "This is what you signed up for" comes in. No one is forcing you to be in a relationship with anyone. Only you decide what relationship you enter, and it is your responsibility to decide if it's a good idea.

Needless to say, we are young. Most of our relationships in the following years are going to be learning experiences that will teach us how to choose the right ones. If you make a decision that isn't great, that is fine. You will make mistakes, someone's feelings will get hurt. So long as you remember to treat others with the same care you'd want to receive during this process, mistakes are fine. Sometimes you're not even going to get that part right but you have to keep trying. Sometimes you'll have to say sorry and sometimes you'll have to decide whether or not you want to listen to someone else's apology to you. My point here is to remind you that you're empowered to make your own decisions. First and foremost, your obligation is to keep yourself safe. So give it all some thought, make an effort to learn about each other, don't rush, and enjoy every experience you have in full.

CHAPTER 8:
FEELINGS AND
COMMUNICATION

To speak freely is to liberate yourself, a liberation that comes only with vulnerability. If you open the door to your home, you trust that your guests won't steal from you, and you don't ask them to unfold their pockets before they leave. In the same way, if you want to communicate well with your partner you can't make them wait outside the door. You must trust them to come inside.

Prior to writing this book, I asked the people around me what their main relationship struggle was. The most common answer was, overwhelmingly, communication. As straightforward as it may seem, communicating with your partner—or with anyone for that matter—is a daunting experience. And, simultaneously one of the most important ones. As teenagers especially, whether we realize it or not, we want to be understood. We want to know we're not alone and that someone, anyone, feels as we feel. Our parents don't seem to understand, our teachers are out of touch, so when our partners don't get us it can feel really frustrating. When we're communicating with our partners, as much as we'd like to hear them, the desire to *be* heard can overwhelm our empathy. More than just being heard, most of us, by protective instinct, want to be right.

Even if you and your partner are both making a sincere effort to communicate to the best of your abilities, you may still find it difficult to comprehend one another's perspective. One reason for this may be a general apprehensiveness to opening up. If one or both partners have been shut down for being vulnerable in the past—being made fun of, ignored, or betrayed after showing their true feelings—they will understandably be hesitant to do so again, no matter how supportive their partner.

The other reason open communication can be frustrating is that each partner has a different style of communication. Our behaviors around communication stem mainly from our childhood, reflecting how we were spoken to and heard, or not heard, growing up. There are four main types of communicators: passive, aggressive, passive-aggressive, and assertive.

The first type, passive communication, is often a learned quality in individuals stemming from abusive partners or family members that trampled over them. It's a place people stay out of fear. Passive communicators may also be referred to as "doormats." They're submissive to their partners and make an effort to avoid any confrontation so as to keep conflict to a minimum. Passive people are often perceived as "easy-going" individuals who are unproblematic *and nice* to be around. In reality, what lies beneath this still surface is a fear of being controversial. Passive communicators genuinely want to keep the peace. It's become ingrained in them that when they have opinions differing from others it is going to cause problems. They've learned that it's better to swallow their true feelings than to make themselves heard.

It's easy to become frustrated at a passive partner's unwillingness to communicate, but be patient with them to the best of your abilities—they are likely just scared of what will happen if they speak up for themselves. A passive person's solution to their own emotions is to try to hide them away, to forget that they have ideas of their own. Passive people won't argue against their partners' decisions, but they also won't always try to lead or solve any problems. This reluctance can place an incredible amount of pressure on their partners to keep the relationship going. Still, as it is with anything regarding love and commitment, a genuine, mutual perseverance for change will birth success.

Aggressive communicators are on the exact opposite side of the spectrum as passive ones. Rather than being overridden by someone else's say, they preemptively override. Their fear comes from the same place as passive communicators. They fear vulnerability, and want to ensure that they continue to feel protected. Aggressive communicators will easily become defensive during conversations, blocking out the feelings of their partner. They want to hear their partners out, but if they are wrong then something is, to them, wrong with them. Fault is indicative of failure. As they are combative, conversations intended to foster open communication will nearly always escalate to an argument. Aggressive communicators are more prone to yelling and using a harsher tone to express their feelings. They are deceptive because all of the power and outward enlargement of themselves is to compensate for how small they really feel, but of course they cannot let you see that. Again, this is a survival technique that stems from some form of abuse. They've been made to feel in the past that they're nothing, they don't matter, that no one cares what they want or who they are. While this has caused their sense of worth to shrink, they try to cover this up by making themselves outwardly large. Even if they don't mean to, their communication style can scare their partners out of expressing themselves, notably passive individuals. They don't mean to scare, they *need* to protect themselves.

If you find yourself in a relationship with an aggressive communicator, do your best to understand their aggression likely comes from some place of feeling smaller and unimportant. Try to remain calm and level-headed, as matching their level of intensity will only escalate things. Choose your words carefully, with emphasis on what positive changes can be made in the situation rather than what's wrong with it currently. If their behavior truly gets out of hand, set boundaries—you can always walk away to show them that's not an appropriate way to treat you. Being in a relationship means finding ways to communicate with your partner even when it's difficult, but it doesn't mean having to be constantly stressed out about speaking to them. Respect them, and respect yourself.

Individuals with a passive-aggressive style of communication are generally the ones most uncomfortable with managing emotions: both theirs and their partner's. They'll tend to communicate their feelings through humor and sarcasm, brushing off the intensity with wit. This style of communication is frustratingly indirect, it's almost as if they're expecting their partner to read their mind. Passive-aggressive communicators claim to be indifferent to most situations, but they'll let you know that's untrue verbally and nonverbally. For example, they may offer to help you with something but then ceaselessly complain about it both during and afterward. The things they do will seem hypocritical and can easily leave their partner feeling like they can't ask them for anything: help, emotional growth, etc.. Regardless of their level of self-awareness, passive-aggressive people are holding years of emotion inside themselves that they cannot quite figure out how to release. Having never been taught how to effectively communicate emotions, the default becomes to stuff them down. They're not sure what to do with themselves, or they are afraid to try. As a partner, be patient with them and do your best to model direct, clear communication, and foster a relationship in which it's okay to say no. If you sense them holding back, ask pointed questions and respond positively to the answers. Set the standard for what healthy emotional expression looks like.

Considered to be the most secure in themselves and their emotions are the assertive communicators. Assertive communicators have a good sense of self-confidence. They're not fearful of expressing their feelings, nor are they afraid of receiving any criticism. They are the most genuinely communicative of the four types. Rather than turning a conversation into an argument, as aggressive communicators do, they do the opposite: their reaction isn't defense but rather to be curious about their partner. Assertive communicators are able to create a calm, cohesive environment for talking. They listen without getting angry and speak their mind without making it a game of whose-fault-is-what. Because of the conditions they set, a conversation doesn't appear as intimidating. These are people who have been lucky enough to have open, loving communication modeled to them from a young age, or who are self-aware enough to have overcome less than ideal conditioning.

Communication is a learned skill and all of our communication styles stem from another part of our life, most often our parents. There's so much you have to learn about yourself and your partner to solidify an effective exchange of feelings. Communication expands beyond the verbal to the non-verbal. The forms in which they come are, well, boundless. Our bodies are constantly communicating our emotions, both consciously and unconsciously, and our brains are incredible at picking up on the slightest change of our partner's tone, inflection, posture, etc. Communicating with your partner can be stressful, especially when you haven't needed to take someone else's feelings into such personal account before. Trust the way the process teeters: the unsteadiness is indicative of change.

Every human is encumbered by the longing to be seen; having a partner means there is someone who is there to bear witness to your life. There is someone who, in every way, can be there to see you fall and rise. You can be completely known by another, but the knowledge will not come about without your permission. Before a conversation with your partner even begins, discern why you're really feeling what you are; seek to know yourself well enough to fairly explain it to them. It's easy to jump to the conclusion that your partner has made a mistake, and much harder to think about how you've contributed to the ensuing result. The guilty feeling we get when we realize something was in fact our fault is sharp and nothing if not an unagreeable sentiment. It makes sense that we put more work into avoiding it than allowing it. However, the way to support your partner is being a partner yourself—being a partner who can hold your mistakes and be okay with having made them. This act of humility fosters a safe environment for mistakes to be made and addressed.

Having a constructive conversation with your partner about what you're both feeling requires patience and intentional empathy. You both have to *want* to listen to each other. If one person checks out of the conversation until it's their turn to talk about everything that's been bothering them, it will be obvious and the conversation will fall apart before it even has a chance to start. No relationship is one-sided; no experience is without multiple perspectives. You should assume they are right before they are wrong. While you speak, keep in mind that the person you're talking to is also another human being with feelings. They can be overwhelmed by what you're saying, whether or not that reaction is justified. Guilt is one of the most unbearable emotions for us, especially when it comes to the people we love. Be intentional in how you phrase your words. Rather than saying, "When you did this," alter it to something more along the lines of, "I felt like this when this happened."

One time, I got into a fight with my long-distance boyfriend because I wasn't doing great at letting him know via text when I had to go do something. He had expressed that it was important for me to tell him when I had to run to class or practice so he wasn't left waiting mid-conversation. I really wanted to help reassure him in this way, but I would be so busy and caught up in my day sometimes I'd forget to tell him my plans and leave in the middle of texting him. He told me that it made it really hard for him to feel like I was thinking about him while being so far away, which I was, but I became so upset because I was already overwhelmed by my busy schedule. The first thing I did was start justifying myself, explaining why it was happening, but I realized quickly that wasn't what I was supposed to be doing at that moment. I was supposed to be saying sorry, owning that I made a mistake and communicating with him so that he could feel more loved and less anxious. In full honesty, I didn't want to say sorry. I was extremely busy and frustrated with my already tiring schedule, so I could have chosen to just argue with him over and over again, but he had expressed a need that I had committed to, so I had to figure it out.

This isn't true 100% of the time, but remember that whatever your partner did, they were probably not trying to hurt you. They care for you deeply and presumably were not aware that their actions would impact you the way that they did. It's aggravating to feel like they don't understand why you're upset, so when the anger starts to come out, take a step back and breathe. You are not being attacked by your partner. Likewise, if you're the one whose partner is sharing something that bothered them, slow down before getting defensive. Is what you're feeling authentic or are you projecting your feelings onto the situation? Whether or not you understand one another in that moment, you are both feeling something that is true on some level. Regardless of what they're saying, offer them the validation they need to feel heard. You don't have to fully understand, but letting them know you're actively listening will help both of you in difficult conversations. This doesn't mean you're just mindlessly accepting what they're saying as right either. Validation does not mean confirmation, it means, "I see you. I'm listening."

Know that you don't have to solve the problem either. Being an active listener for your partner does not mean you're accepting some sort of defeat. If you believe, after considering all perspectives of the conversation, that you're not in the wrong, voice that. You may find later that you did actually do something and in that case come back, let your ego down, apologize and move past it. Pride will only hold you back in love: your goal is not to be above your partner but counterparts.

Most people would choose to be right and upset than wrong and happy. If in a conversation you feel overwhelmed or see that you can longer view the situation clearly, take some space. Do not run away though, there's a difference. Running away from a conversation means leaving when you no longer want to hear the other person's point of view. Taking space is rather understanding when you cannot support the comfortable, listening environment that you and your partner have created to talk. If you feel this way, clearly and calmly let your partner know you need a moment to come back to yourself, and you'll resume the conversation as soon as you can do so fairly. You don't need to get it right the first time, you just need to be committed to trying it again.

We aren't born with perfect communication skills. The first way we know to express ourselves in this world is to cry, hit, and ball up on the floor. Communication goes against a safety mechanism in our minds. In order to prevent us from feeling hurt or threatened, the first thing our brain does is protect our own feelings. Improving your communication is uncomfortable, but it is a pillar in the foundation of a solid relationship.

CHAPTER 9: TRIGGERS AND INSECURITIES

Who we are, who we become, must start from somewhere. Triggers and insecurities, although each with their own distinctions, share a familiar origin: one of our prior experiences in this world. Frequently, those experiences were one of our firsts. For example, what happens in our first platonic and romantic relationships sets a precedent for how we interact with and view the rest of them. Despite our best efforts, the most tender parts of ourselves always claim a large role in our bonds, often in ways we'd wish them not to.

We see the word "trigger" in loud, bold print every so often when scrolling through Twitter or Instagram, but what does it really mean? Simply put, a trigger is defined as something that causes a traumatic memory to resurface. When triggered, a person is pulled from the present into a painful moment from their past. Triggers manifest in both obvious and more subtle ways. Sometimes they're easy to see, sometimes not, with reactions from yelling or crying to shutting down to just looking a little uncomfortable. One of my old schoolmates was swarmed by red ants as a child, so now he cannot stand to be near them. Despite the somewhat humorous nature of the event, he has a legitimate trigger now and steers clear of any insect. While his was caused by a singular event, this is not necessarily always the case. Much more often, triggers stem from a pattern of mistreatment—usually from unhealthy constants rooted in our own home.

Many of our triggers develop from our family. Even if you grew up with loving, attentive parents, you will still pick up the good and the bad of them. The way we were treated growing up gives us a model for how we think the world will interact with us. Children who grew up with dismissive, inattentive parents expect the world to disregard them. In any instance when that expectation proves true, those individuals are being returned to the state of their youth. To a young boy who was yelled at and put down all his childhood years, harsh, disciplinary tones probably have a greater impact on him than if his experience had been different. To a girl who grew up being praised for being pretty rather than being smart or kind, any criticism of her appearance will throw her off much more than it would someone else. Our childhood years are so formative for us since our parents are our first kind of relationship, so we carry these presuppositions with us throughout our entire lives.

As you grow and start to experience your first romantic relationships, you will realize that the greatest loves are capable of fostering an equally intense pain. The more you love someone, the larger your capacity for resenting or being disappointed in them. Anything your partner does is significantly more impactful to you than the actions of a friend. Because of this massive effect they have on you, the lines between an actual attack or criticism from your partner and a trigger become instantly blurred if you're not consciously looking for the difference. These triggers creep through the harmless, common, or even playful parts of a relationship to try and pull you back to a familiar pain. Thus, the ability to differentiate what is real and what is a projection of an old experience is the first step to being less susceptible to your past.

When we become triggered, our subconscious attempts to protect us by swaddling us in one of four responses: fight, flight, freeze, or fawn. Evolutionarily, our bodies have evolved so that in moments of danger—say, if there was something chasing us —every resource we have to keep us alive automatically kicks in. Our heart rate picks up, pumping more blood to our muscles so we can run faster and fight better. Adrenaline floods the body so we have more energy, then our pupils dilate to let more light in to temporarily improve our eyesight.

This is all necessary when we're fighting off a threat, but not what we need when we're emotionally triggered. However our brains function in the same manner to this imagined threat, and all the same responses kick in.

Some people are immediately prone to the fight response, exerting force when they're triggered. They may yell at you or try to physically protect themselves. Others take flight, leaving the situation entirely alone. Some, often those who have been in abusive situations, freeze up and disassociate in an effort to remove themselves from the discomfort of the situation—much in the way passive communicators do. The fawning response is different from the others. Rather than trying to protect themselves by getting bigger or smaller, those who fawn try to appease those who triggered them. They believe that to gratify the aggressor is to pacify them. They make a bargain, exchanging affection for safety.

None of these responses make for a comfortable environment for either partner. The individual that becomes easily triggered will be compulsively untrusting of their partner and the other will be afraid of doing anything in the present that might resemble the past. That's not to say triggers are not normal and cannot exist in a relationship. We all have triggers. As with anything, it is about how both members of a relationship respond to it.

How do you know when you're feeling triggered, and how can you shift your reaction to it? There are moments when elevated emotions are definitely valid, and it can be hard to differentiate between appropriate reactions to the here and now, and overblown reactions based on the past. In order to recognize when a trigger is in fact a trigger, you need to be able to rewind the moment. Your first reaction to being triggered will be something against your partner. Following your fight, flight, freeze, or fawn instinct will be tempting, but don't fall for it. You are scared so your brain is going to do anything to keep you safe, but you don't have to keep employing old solutions. Don't say anything at first, just sit with whatever it is. Identify what situation in the past could be making this moment so difficult for you. Would this have bothered you if the traumatic event that happened a couple years or months ago hadn't happened? Is your actual partner trying to hurt you in this moment? When you feel triggered, keep yourself grounded in trust. Trust that you are okay and that you won't let something hurt you. And, trust the person who cares for you that's sitting in front of you. If it helps, hold their hands, feel them, remember who they are and who they are not. They are not the person from your past.

Trust is a decision you have to make. You have to make the choice to trust someone every day. I understand that sounds almost disrespectful to ask of you. How can you just choose to trust someone when you've been hurt? You have to be cautious and you're not even trying to have these walls up. It feels impossible, it probably feels entirely out of your control.

Prior to dating my partner you know as Riley, I was in a dynamic with someone in which I felt very used. I felt I was valued solely for the body I had, nothing more. So when Riley would say things that my previous partner had said during intimate moments, I took flight. I got anxious and would shut myself off from him, avoiding his calls and texts for a little while. It wasn't Riley's fault, he loved me and the intention behind his words was entirely different than those of my previous partner. However, that didn't stop me from feeling the need to defend myself. Hearing those same words triggered me in such a way that I was put right back in a room, sitting with my ex, feeling used and unimportant. It was a lot of pressure on Riley to be there for me with all of the distance between us that I created. I would tell him I was trying to trust him, and that was true, but he insisted it was a decision I would have to make. Every time he would give me this *order* (as I perceived it), I thought how dare he speak to my trauma, but I came to understand that he was right, it was a choice. It was a choice I hadn't been ready to make, because it's a horrifying choice. So from then on, every time I felt triggered I would stop and say out loud, "I trust you." To this day, and I'm sure for many more, I still have to make that decision with everyone I meet. Most times I make that decision, it doesn't come naturally, but I've learned that in this case, what comes naturally isn't in my best interest. Sometimes challenging your own judgement is the best thing you can do for yourself.

The act of staying conscious of what's actually going on in these moments is the most important aspect of moving forward. If your trigger comes out in the form of you lashing out at your partner, apologize. It is a good partner's joy to help you evolve, but it's not their responsibility to receive the things you want to say to the people who have actually hurt you. Your partner should be understanding of your triggered moments if you communicate them effectively. However, if your triggers consistently impact them and you're not making progress in addressing them— whether intentionally or not—it's important to acknowledge how it is affecting them. It isn't always easy to see our blind spots, so do your best to stay present with their feelings and listen to them instead of responding with your first reaction. You don't need to feel guilty for having triggers, we all have them.

As you explore your triggers and become more self-aware, don't be afraid to talk to your partner about your triggers during and even before they come up. Your vocalization is more productive for the two of you than your silence. Your partner *wants* to hear you. Not only does it let them know when you're triggered and in need of their support, but it can also help *them* know how to avoid reviving old patterns. As you share these things with your partner, tell them about your story, not about their faults. Your past is not your fault, but it is not their fault either.

As difficult as it can be to experience your own trigger, it's just as overwhelming to be the partner taking on someone else's past. If this is you, be patient and empathetic while your partner works through trauma. If they're panicking and don't realize they're responding to something outside of their real situation, it's okay to help them recognize it in a supportive way. Don't yell, and don't shame them. Gently offer the idea that they could be triggered. Then, if they seem willing, talk through it with them. You will figure out how comfortable they are talking about certain things, but don't be afraid to ask questions about their past. Together, you may even be able to bring some levity to the situation. Maybe you two can make light of and joke about their triggers to use humor as a means to move on. It can be a friendly way to acknowledge it, but respect that not everyone is ready for that yet. Our past can be a very heavy burden for us. Sometimes being reminded that our experience was authentic and not something we need to feel ashamed of is all we need.

Our pasts reveal more about us than just our triggers, but also our insecurities. Everyone feels insecure in some way, whether it's intellectually, physically, financially, socially, about their own value or personality, and so on. Everyone is struggling with something, and relationships facilitate our insecurities just as much as they do our fears. Insecurities stem from many of the same sources as triggers do: a lack of family support, past failures, perfectionism, social anxiety. As teenagers we don't wholly know who we are yet. We shed layers while we experiment with ourselves. We aren't secure in our own identity, and all of the discovering comes with sometimes not liking who we are in that process.

Insecurities, just like triggers, dwell inside sadness or anger, with a tendency to bloom into resentment. The feeling of inadequacy surfaces in relationships when someone feels like they're undeserving of their partner, or love at all for that matter. Feeling unworthy of the person you care about comes from another experience where somehow it was proven to them that they didn't deserve something. Maybe with a family member or past partner they weren't made to feel sufficient no matter what they did. Maybe they had overly strict parents or were cheated on by someone they were with. When someone's main goal becomes trying to meet their parents' standards as a child, but they never receive any validation, they tend to overly crave it in relationships. Or, they avoid relationships altogether by staying in that headspace that they'll never be good enough. Likewise, if in a past relationship an individual's partner told them they were annoying, not smart enough, too emotional, not trying hard enough, or were just constantly loading them with negative feedback, they will feel more distant from deserving good love. It will feel out of reach.

The most difficult part of trying to move past insecurity is the mental game of convincing yourself that you do deserve better, or that you are attractive, strong, or smart enough. Especially with the countless images we are presented with from society and social media, we must actively keep convincing ourselves that we are not lacking. Pay attention to your day-to-day internal dialogue. How are you speaking about yourself in your own head? In stressful situations, are you putting yourself down? It can be even simpler than that in the way you talk to yourself about the little things. What's your first thought when you accidentally forget to do something or you didn't wake up with your hair looking the way you wanted it to? If you can begin catching yourself in the act of indulging in overly critical thoughts, force yourself to stop right then. It may sound ridiculous but you can correct yourself in your own head. If you call yourself stupid, you can pause and say to yourself, "That's actually not really true, is it?" This is a practice just between you and yourself, no one is going to be judging you. You'll get better at it with intention too; your thoughts are powerful, and are best guarded with care. The little things that we normalize in our day are what end up having the broadest impact.

In relationships, people with consuming insecurities show up in very distinct ways that can, on the surface, just seem somewhat annoying or dramatic. A person's flimsy sense of security in themselves drives their anxiety. Often people with these feelings keep busy. They tend to be always doing something, always running around or working on something. To compensate for the validation they are incapable of giving themselves, they'll try to find it in others by doing anything to please them. Not having a strong sense of self-worth can easily manifest into forms of jealousy and distrust of a partner. It's hard for them to allow their partner to be with other people, and even if they do, they'll seek constant communication.

Retroactive jealousy—feeling jealous of someone's past partners and experience—is not uncommon either, especially as a teenager. Retroactive jealousy occurs more often in relationships where there is a significant difference in the partners' levels of dating experience. While it makes sense to feel a bit insecure if your partner is more experienced than you, your lack of experience is not something they should be punished for (nor is it something you yourself should be ashamed of). In truth, any insecurities around self-worth are not our partner's fault, and attacking or punishing them for it will only, in the end, push them away. Our relationships aggravate our insecurities, and unhealthy ones often amplify them. Even so, while they are something you should be able to communicate to your partner, they are still yours to own. Any of this jealousy or insecurity doesn't mean someone is bad or ridiculous. Don't think of it as a character flaw, but rather as an open wound. As with most things, it's the responsibility of both partners to be open to growth so that the wounds of both individuals may heal and not spread.

Even in a solid, well-functioning relationship, anyone can still have the fear of rejection. Sometimes partners will be afraid of asking for help, support, or truly just anything at all. I've personally struggled with this where I didn't feel confident enough to ask for anything unless my partner pried it out of me.

When I took a closer look at my insecurities, I realized that I hadn't been unworthy of the things I wanted, I had just been taught by other people that it wasn't okay to ask for them. Once I found its source, I was able to remind myself in the present that this was a different reality, and that I had the freedom to move forward and be more aware of my instincts so as to be able to change them. You can reprogram these responses in the same way you would with a physical trauma. Feel the wound, address it at its point of origin, and disengage that from the present.

Never stop talking in a relationship. Constant vulnerability and transparency is frightening; it is also the practice that ensures you and your partner are both held accountable. You can validate yourself, acknowledge your triggers when you feel unworthy. However, while you shouldn't solely depend on your partner to keep your head above water, they are still a resource for you to depend upon. Know too that you cannot reprogram your partner's triggers or fix their insecurities yourself, even by providing them with all the affirmations and stability you can muster. They must also work to discover it for themselves. We all have triggers and insecurities. As we are all human, we all bear the impacts of these struggles, and benefit from the strengths they may bring. But by becoming more aware of them (and your reactions to them), you allow yourself the opportunity to heal the past to help you sustain a healthier relationship with both your partner and yourself.

CHAPTER 10:
EXPLORING INTIMACY

B eneath the surface of our bodies is a system that powers itself in synchronicity with all of its moving parts: the brain and the body work together to heal, adapt, and sustain life. Every cell contributes collectively to this network, ensuring life continues to flow through us. Millions of signals pulse constantly through the nervous system, coordinating processes and reactions. Cells regenerate, tissues repair, and organs collaborate, each reporting to the other. The body is as resilient as it is smart. However, with the meticulous relationship it has with itself also comes a sensitivity to the world. The body knows more about us than we do. It becomes imprinted by all of our experiences. It remembers everything, every seemingly insignificant bump and bruise, every touch—it holds much more than we're consciously aware of.

Cautiousness thus limits the contusions. By remembering past injuries and adjusting its responses to avoid further harm, the body is able to adapt and protect itself. And so, deciding who you share your body with for the first time is (intelligently) nerve-racking. The question of when and how to start exploring intimacy and sex has a different answer for everybody. You could feel ready as soon as you start dating or you may like the idea of waiting a few years better. There is no right time to start being intimate. There's no rush nor any obligation you have to anybody. Your only obligation is to yourself, to make the decision that is best for you. Taking the time to understand your own needs and boundaries first is a way of respecting the system your body has cultivated to protect your emotional and physical well-being.

When you're starting to consider any form of intimacy, make sure your reasons for doing so are for yourself. In its purest form, being intimate with someone is a way to bring the relationship closer, to explore each other on another level. It's an opportunity to be vulnerable and to be seen in a new way you haven't before. And more simply, it can just be a fun, enjoyable thing to share with someone else. If these are your true motivations, you're on the right track. However, if you're saying yes to going beyond kissing because you feel bad that you're taking away from your partner's experience, or because all your friends are doing it, or you're just too old not to have done anything yet, take a step back and reevaluate what is going on for *you*. Everyone has different reasons for exploring their sexuality, just make sure it is what you actually want to be doing. Wanting to experiment is not wrong, nor is the desire for intimacy something to be dismissed.

Regardless of what your reasons are, choosing a partner to explore intimacy with is a process that should be taken with some care. Physical intimacy may not even be something you or your partner are ready for or even thinking about. You may just want to date and have fun without stepping into that. If you do decide to become intimate, you want to be with someone you can trust, both during the experience and in what they will do afterward. In high school especially, gossip is more powerful than any amount of sincerity. Everyone likes to talk—it's a natural way of social grooming and discovering our status in our communities. However, this experimentation can at times end up being harmful. Information gives us power over the knowledge of the public. The more we know the more interesting our conversations seem to become. We're all experiencing things we never have before, so we want to share those discoveries with everyone, or we are talking about someone else to make sense of ourselves. But, as I'm sure we can all relate to, the effect this can have on how someone is perceived is powerful.

The excitement we feel as teenagers when experiencing our firsts in the world is wonderful, and our natural inclination to share those moments with someone is equally a part of that beauty. Nevertheless, it is something to be aware of as you step into intimacy. If you're in a committed relationship, and even if you're not, make an effort to have a conversation about who you will share any details of your experiences with. This can be tough to bring up (which is another reason to have a partner you can trust), but you'll always be thankful you did so in the end. An arrangement I've made with my past partner is that we didn't share our private experiences with anyone but each other. Create straightforward parameters that make the both of you feel comfortable and strictly hold yourself to that expectation. Telling even one more person on a whim could feel harmless to you, but doing that could break a strong sense of common trust between you and your partner.

When you do decide that you're ready to be intimate, it doesn't necessarily mean your partner will be ready as well. When you communicate with them that you're ready to go further, be open and accepting of whatever their feelings are. They may be ready too, or they may be scared. If so, open up a transparent conversation. Sometimes, fear of intimacy may come not from a lack of readiness, but from worries about body anxiety or just fear of not being able to do whatever it is you want very well. If you sense this is the case with your partner, it's okay to give them some gentle motivation to try more, but there's a difference between pressure and motivation. Motivation is a gentle nudge that supports someone to step outside their comfort zone and explore what feels intimidating. Pressure, on the other hand, pushes them into something they're not ready for, ignoring their hesitation and choice. If they do blatantly state, in any way, that they are not ready, prepared, or wanting to be intimate physically, that is the end of the conversation. In certain cases, people just have specific values about intimacy and at what point of their life they experience it, which is also something deserving of respect. Regardless of the fact that you may desperately want to be intimate with them, it is not the right time for them. If the idea does resurface, allow it to be initiated by them.

Oftentimes, partners will have had different levels of experience when it comes to intimacy. Especially when dating someone older, your partner may know more than you do. This may feel intimidating at first, but take it to your own advantage. You have someone who can guide you through learning and teach you new things. On the other hand, if your partner is inexperienced and chooses you to be there for the first time for any aspect of intimacy, you take on the responsibility of guiding them. You're the only thing they know yet. Be patient with your partner and allow room for humor and kindness. You may not be able to see it, but they're probably very scared. The expectation for you in this moment is to be a guardian of their body. Remember that the body keeps everything: if you are the first to hold it, it will know your touch forever.

Being intimate with a new partner brings, with every experience, the rediscovery of intimacy itself. You will both have different preferences and what your ex may have loved, they may really not enjoy. Throughout experimenting, keep the conversation going. Frequent check-ins of simply asking, "Yes or no?" go a long way. During moments of intimacy, let your connection settle into a natural cadence, where your movements complement the other. But be mindful not to overwhelm your partner with constant questioning; too many words can disrupt this rhythm and bring it to a halt. And as much as you ask, tell. If something is uncomfortable for you, saying you need an adjustment is not a turn-off, it's communication. If you try to mask your discomfort, your experience pivots to inauthentic. Even if you're trying to make things easier, it will still make it less enjoyable for you both. Nakedness doesn't necessarily mean vulnerability or intimacy. You can be touched and remain hidden at the same time. The authentic experience will always be the better one, and it will always be the true one.

When it comes to giving and receiving, don't assume you know what your partner prefers, and don't expect them to read your mind either. While each of you both giving and receiving pleasure during intimacy makes the entire experience most fulfilling, certain people may prefer to only either give pleasure or receive it. The relinquishing of control over their own body when receiving pleasure can make some people feel extremely defenseless. Some feel guilty about the absence of servicing their partner. On the other hand, certain people may feel anxious about their ability to give pleasure to their partner and therefore avoid it. For others it's simply more fun to give than to receive. Point being, there are a thousand reasons behind people's preferences, so it is important to understand what it is your partner wants.

Figure out what feels good for both of you, together, and help your partner learn. Know that you're deserving of such pleasure too. If you have trouble giving, a helpful thought to keep in the back of your mind is that by your actions, you have the ability to make your partner almost incapacitated by how good they feel. You hold the power in that moment. There is great pleasure to be found—physically, as well as mentally and emotionally—in both giving and receiving. If the idea of this power is just as intimidating, think about the care you're giving them. They are letting you in and you get to take care of their body.

As you start to feel more comfortable with who you are and begin to share that with someone else, you may start to think about the next layer of intimacy: sex. It's normal to feel a mix of excitement and nervousness. Just remember, the right time is when *you* feel ready—not when someone else asks. Take your time, listen to what your body wants, and trust that you'll know when the moment feels right for you. The very word "sex" can feel intimidating and overwhelming, in both good ways and bad, and it is. It's the first time you're fully revealed to another person, laying bare your entire physical self—which is possibly the most vulnerable position to put yourself in as a human being. Sex helps to complete a partnership, but it's not necessary to be close with someone if it's not what you want.

No one can tell you when you're ready for this experience. In fact, you may find that your mind feels ready but your body isn't. That is perfectly okay. You want to wait to have sex until it doesn't even feel like something you need to question anymore. When you're ready, it should come with ease. In my moment of realization, I recall feeling a sudden ripple of stillness, detached from the questions of right or wrong, which were replaced by a new, acute awareness of the unlikely beauties of the world. I recall noticing the sublime way the room was kindly illuminated by the daylight, how the air was thick with the faithful warmth of the sun. I was gifted a new awareness that everything around me was simplistically fashioned to perfection. In that moment, I existed infinitely in the safeguard of my partner. All was calm. All was quiet. All was right.

There is so much to consider before having sex. Who you're doing it with, the potential consequences, how to do it safely and when. When it comes to choosing who your first will be, you're much more likely to have an enjoyable experience if it's with someone you know well enough to be comfortable with, and to trust. Having sex for the first time on a one-night stand may sound thrilling, but I would strongly recommend otherwise. From my own experience, I would suggest waiting for a serious, long-term partner or in some cases, a very close friend, which provides you a baseline of security for this experience. Experiencing your first time with someone you're close friends with can release much of the pressure, in such a way permissing the playfulness to eclipse the seriousness. Being intimate like this is not the same as a first kiss. It is a full disclosure of your body, so don't treat it as if it's a task you need to get done.

It's just as important to think about *how* you do it as it is to think about who you're doing it with. While you don't want to lose the fun and excitement of this first moment of intimacy, a little bit of planning around the circumstances of the night and morning after your first time can go a long way. These times surrounding the experience are just as important as the experience itself. You might feel very aware of your nakedness after your first time. If you go home 20 minutes after losing your virginity, you will feel emptier instead of more fulfilled. Where will you be for your first time and will you have time to be together afterward? Bring up these questions with your partner and make a plan. I know it doesn't sound like the most enjoyable conversation, but it will serve to remove half the stress later on. What's more, you will ensure you don't miss out on the tenderness that the moments after your first time bring.

While planning can lessen the anxiety of it all, sometimes that first experience isn't planned. Things like creating a whole set up and wearing elaborate lingerie can help your first time feel special, but it's not at all necessary. The spark of spontaneity can be just what is needed to make it memorable. In which case, the only thing you should be focusing on at that moment is, again, whether or not it feels right.

The most important thing during, before, and after sex is to keep communication going. While some of these conversations may feel uncomfortable, it's nothing compared to the discomfort of something happening that you're not prepared for. If your partner has already had experience, it's not overbearing and is, rather, in your best interest to ask them if they have any STDs. If your partner's answer is yes, it doesn't necessarily mean you cannot or should not have sex with them, the decision is just now yours to make. It's your right to know if they have a disease you could contract and under no circumstance is it acceptable for a partner to withhold that information from you.

Talk about your preferred uses of contraception. Know that you each may have different ideas about how you want to do it, and that's normal and *why* you talk it through. Your partner may say it's okay not to use condoms, and if you disagree you do not have to change your mind. If they respect you, they'll respect your decision. Girls, if you have access to birth control that's always an option as well. It can be comforting to have this extra level of protection against pregnancy, but know it doesn't protect against STDs. Also know the hormones in these pills can have a serious effect on your body, so never feel pressured to go on the pill if it's not something you want to do for yourself.

While most schools make students attend sexual health and STD courses, oftentimes these courses are awkward and unwelcoming so you certainly don't need to be dependent on them. Give yourself the courtesy of looking online or asking someone close to you about it on your own. Education empowers you to be more comfortable with your rights to consent and helps you be more aware of how to go about things safely and healthily.

Having unprotected or protected sex is a personal decision for each couple, although I am in no way advocating for having unprotected engagements. By default, use a condom. Condoms can be confusing and there's a lot more to them than there may seem. Make sure it's on the right way—condoms can be on inside out and the size does matter. There comes a risk with them being too small or too big. Guys, take it upon yourself to find the right size for you and girls, ensure your partner understands the importance of paying attention to it. Never rely on just your partner for checking for any holes or tears, to feel fully confident check it yourself. If your partner is more advanced than you, it can be comforting to let them take the lead, but at the same time make sure to ask questions so you understand what's going on. Learn how to put one on yourself no matter your biological sex so you can be fully aware of the process. As always, communication will make the whole thing go so much smoother. This can be a lot to have to think about. In the beginning it can feel really overwhelming, but over time these things become less like a to-do list and will just feel like a natural part of the process.

It's also important to be aware of and understand the conventional aspects of sex in your particular location, i.e. the legal age of sex in your state. These ideas may seem tedious and obvious, but you want to be informed so there's no panic later on. Look up the legal age of sex where you are and understand that even with no ill intentions, having sex with a minor if you're of age and even only one year their senior, or vice versa, could potentially cause an issue down the line. Also take into serious account that, if you're a hetero couple, there is a possibility of pregnancy, even when you're taking measures against it. On that note, review the abortion laws in your state, if that is a path your beliefs align with. It can be helpful too to talk with your partner about what you would want to do if pregnancy did occur. While thinking about these things beforehand may seem like overkill, it's always better to prepare together than be potentially blindsided.

I won't get into the technical aspect of sex, but I can speak to a few physical things you shouldn't feel surprised about later. For my female readers (although no discouragement to men who want to further educate themselves), before having sex for the first time, I was terrified of the pain. In videos (and let us be candid, we've all looked there to make sense of things at some point), you see girls screaming or crying, which doesn't create a great first expectation for what's supposed to be one of the most influential experiences of your life. Your first time, and quite a few times after that, it will initially be uncomfortable and you may even feel a strong stinging sensation. I won't sugarcoat it: for the first 20 seconds or so, it can be quite painful. However, if you do your best to keep your focus on breathing, giving into the tension rather than tensing up, those 20 seconds of discomfort will break and you will find release. Those first moments can feel intimidating though; you may start panicking and worry that it won't go away, that you're going to be stuck in that feeling of distress. If you need to end there, that's fine. Breathe. Baby steps, baby steps, baby steps. During those moments of stress breathe deeply and intentionally, tell yourself it will pass and maybe even try laughing about something in the meantime. It may seem counterintuitive to laugh in this uncomfortable moment, but women's bodies can relax through vocalization, and adding onto that vulnerability that you two can share makes all the difference. It can be a sign to you and your partner that, "This is difficult, but I know we're going to get through it together."

If you've passed the hard part of those first uncomfortable few times and it still doesn't feel good, a couple things may be going on. Your mind or body may not be ready, or it is not the right position for your body. Try a few different ways and take it very slow. Both partners should be kind and patient for one another the entire time. After you two are done, use the bathroom (you should do this every time to avoid a UTI), and if you are bleeding slightly don't panic. It's normal and you'll be just fine.

Porn can give everyone unrealistic expectations. Even though porn is male-orientated, that doesn't mean it won't impact how men think about themselves. In fact, that focus itself can further anxieties for men in the same way it does for women. Porn often portrays specific expectations of male size and physicality. Most videos online present the audience with two individuals with distinct body types having aggressive and fast sex, but that's not what sex always looks like. And, even when it does look like that, that is not the full picture. Speaking to my male readers from my own experience and that of my friends, your partner is likely far less concerned with your physicality or how long the experience may last, and more with how connected and caring you are with them. Try to let that be the focus of your first time.

The first time isn't usually on a bed of roses, in the perfect outfit with you looking the best you've ever looked. Don't worry if it wasn't everything you were expecting too. For many people, women specifically, pleasure doesn't come until after a lot of experimenting and practice. Sex is a messy process but that's why the right person sets the good experiences apart from the bad. The first time isn't always fireworks, if it's just kind of uncomfortable and intense that's okay. Even if your first time having sex with this person didn't go as planned, if you two can laugh about it and commit to smiling through it together, that's more important than the sex itself.

Always remember that sex is *supposed to be fun* and feel *good*. Keep your mindset light. You get to try new things and some ways are not going to work, where all you can do is laugh about it. Laughter, I will never be able to stress it enough, is indispensable to the human psyche when sharing your body. Find humor in what doesn't work how you thought it would. Again, one of the main things to keep in mind is that sex is not like porn. You may consider that to be obvious, however I promise it has been deeply ingrained into your subconscious. Both partners need to be aware about how they mimic and expect sex to be from the internet. Don't assume your partner will be loud and animated; not everyone expresses their pleasure like this—and don't assume what you saw online is what you're supposed to be doing. Some people do respond very vocally, but many are much quieter and that is simply their natural response to pleasure. What an actor may have seemed to love in porn may, and is probably not, what your partner wants during sex.

A simple solution: ask them what they want. Start with a blank slate. For girls, but also to any gender, sex is *for you*, not an experience that is created by the *use* of you. You're not an entertainer, you are there to enjoy it. If you don't want to make any noise during sex, don't make any noise. Sex is not a performance, it's an interweaving of two people. Guys, if you're having sex with a girl, remember the position it puts a woman in. Your experience is external while a girl's is internal; they are inviting you inside of them. It is an easily fear- and anxiety-inducing experience if not done with care. You don't need to stress yourself out the entire time, but be aware and make sure you are both enjoying it. For girls it can be a lot more difficult to feel pleasure during sex, while it's naturally easier for you. Don't forget to balance the pleasure of both of you in the midst of your cravings.

There should always be tenderness after any sort of intimacy. Aftercare comes in many different forms. For example, showering together after sex is a great way to wind back down and take care of each other. Besides the fact that it's refreshing, it's also another good way for women to avoid UTIs. Sex is wonderful but simultaneously a huge amount of physical exertion. You can't go wrong with something to satiate yourself with after and a big glass of ice water.

After your first time, particularly for girls, you're especially fragile and aftercare is the best way to feel taken care of. Going on your phone after sex could be your first instinct; however be aware of how it may make your partner feel. Seeing you switch focus so quickly can be interpreted by them as you not caring about them or what just happened. If your partner has a tendency to do this, talk with them about it. Let them know how it makes you feel and offer an alternative way to keep being intimate after sex. Staying physically close and cuddling once you two are done is the easiest and for many, the most enjoyable part of aftercare.

In our culture, sex is everywhere. We grow up exposed to countless opinions and a dizzying variety of depictions, and as a result, it can be easy to get lost in someone else's point of view. Media tells us sex is supposed to look and be understood in a certain way. In many cultures, sex is muted and shamed. I had a close friend who felt like she could never talk about her sex life because she had grown up in a deeply religious household where intimacy meant you were dishonoring yourself. While everyone has the right to their own values and opinions, sex should not be seen as a stain on your character. Having sex does not make you anything less nor does it mean you are deserving of shame. Any experience you have is a legitimate one. If you like women as a woman and lose your virginity to one, that is a valid first experience. As is having any other sort of experience that you feel someone else may critique. Sex is something you own for yourself, it doesn't belong to anyone else but you, so you should have it in the way that makes you feel happy and you should take care of it.

CHAPTER 11: STAYING OR LEAVING

The only thing that matches the ferocity of love is the weight of fear. Fear will always grapple with love, and it is the very presence of fear that calls forth love's forbearance. Fear also often takes upon itself the role of the agent of doubt, driving one's choice of whether to stay in or leave a relationship. And often, it looks and feels exactly the same as love does: intoxicating, all-consuming, binding. They're both forces that are, perhaps vainly, relentless in keeping what they want. Leaving someone is then an absolute disruption of the system. Making a choice to leave someone you love is made to feel impossible. Just like falling into love, it is another leap of faith into the opaque. You need to trust that when you let go of their hand, you won't fall apart. Even when you find your footing without them, it's natural to feel unsteady for a while, but that feeling will pass. Ending a relationship means tearing apart the familiar reality your body and mind have grown used to. Even when it's the right choice for your future, your body doesn't necessarily know that. Your mind may not know that either. All they understand is that they're experiencing the removal of something they have become attached to.

That being said, how can you know it's time to leave? How can you tell when familiarity has overshadowed well-being? Start with a simpler question: Why do you get into relationships? Why do you choose to form such a bond, invest your time and energy, and maybe even fall in love with someone? Is it to have someone to share every victory and loss with, to have someone who can brush the dirt off your shoulders and make sure you keep going? Is it that you want someone to be messy around, someone to recognize the beautiful parts of you? All of these questions can be reduced to an even more plain one: Do you get into relationships to make your life better? With that question in mind, *is* being with your partner right now making your life better?

Is life easier with them around or is it exceptionally more difficult? Do you have more things to worry about or less? When you reflect on your relationship, what is there? Distress or calmness, richness or lack, tenderness or indifference?

Recall now the four keys of a thriving relationship from the first chapter: growth, empathy, communication, forgiveness. You should see all of these qualities in your relationship. You two may have some issues that need resolving. In fact I guarantee you do, no relationship is without them. Be that as it may, those issues should be ones that you are both worth working through, and that have the potential to be worked through. If the issue is that your partner has been unfaithful, perhaps the answer to that problem is already clear to you. You should be confident that, as a team, as a unit, you two can carry the weight of these issues together. It should be clear that you are both willing and ready to put forth the effort to make positive changes that will benefit both of your lives.

Your relationship stops when the growth stops. Of the four keys, growth is the root that binds them all. It should have no end. Neither of you should be the person you first met. The hope should be that you are both evolving and becoming better versions of yourself, together. Your partner should bring out the best of you, not draw out the most of your frustration or sadness. Undeniably, at times love brings out the worst in us. But should you love yourself less when you're with someone, they are not the one whose hand you should be holding as you walk through this life. Relationships provide us with an opportunity to learn more about who we are. Your relationship should allow you to peek into aspects of your being you may have forgotten existed. You should be remembering the effervescent playfulness that was once your entire vantage point. And with this reconnection to your most pure, carefree childhood self, your relationships should simultaneously rouse you to embrace the resilience, broader perspective, empathy, and responsibility of adulthood.

If growth is lacking in your relationship, it can prevent you from becoming a more authentic version of yourself. It's natural to discover new aspects of who you are that might not align with your current relationship, and it's okay to embrace those changes. Relationships are parts of our lives that help shape us, but not all of them are meant to stay the same forever. Personal evolution doesn't mean you *have* to leave your wonderful, healthy relationship; however, when it's time for a shift, it's okay to evolve and allow yourself the space to grow into who you're becoming. That's an unreliable thought because, of course, you have no idea what will be on the other side. This is when the trust returns, in the future and in yourself. We are still teenagers with unanswered questions about who we are and where we belong. In answering these questions, the right place for us to be in life will shift. Ultimately, whether for personal growth or simply because you're no longer enjoying the relationship, it's important to recognize when it's time to move on.

On the basis of communication, the talking should never stop. Your needs and wants in your relationship have to be something you can express to your partner. You should feel like you can share everything that is important to you with them. What makes you feel good, what hurts you, what you want to do with your life. You should feel comfortable with your partner being involved.

In addition to communication, when deciding whether to stay in your relationship, it's important to reflect on what role empathy and forgiving are playing in it. Right now, what is the role of empathy and kindness in your relationship? Are you both actively looking out for one another's needs and putting in the effort to help each other improve? Are you consistently trying to be kind, soft, and empathetic, even when things aren't perfect? What feelings do you want to be present in your relationships? Are you both trying to be active participants in the bettering of your relationship or is one of you always looking for a new reason to fight? Do you both want empathy and ease in your relationships or do you want outlets for anger and drama? Are you trying to find a middle ground? Are you choosing to react to any arguments with grace or with the intention of furthering the fire? Relationships take work, and it's easy for things to feel like they're not clicking. But if empathy and kindness are at the core of what you're both bringing to the table, it can make a world of difference in how you approach those tough moments. So, take a moment to ask yourself—are you both committed to those values, even when things get rough?

Furthermore, what are you forgiving, and what are you not? Are you forgiving in a way that helps the relationship grow, or are there things being held onto that create emotional distance? Maybe you're forgiving too much, or perhaps not enough—sometimes we're either too quick to let things go and set boundaries or, on the flip side, we can hold grudges without realizing it. The key here is always keeping the balance. Are you both truly letting go of past mistakes in a healthy way, or are unresolved issues looming? What does forgiveness look like in your relationship, and is it working for both of you? More importantly, is it good for both of you? These questions are here to show you whether you're moving forward together, or if certain things are keeping you stuck. Understanding how empathy, kindness, and forgiveness play into your relationship will give you a clearer sense of whether this relationship can continue to evolve, or if it's time to reconsider what's best for both of you.

If, after the initial excitement fades, you and your partner find yourselves overly reliant on each other, neglecting other aspects of your lives, your relationship may be leaning towards codependency. While it's normal for couples, especially in high school, to spend a lot of time together, healthy relationships maintain a balance between the couple's connection and the wider world. Codependent partners, however, prioritize each other to the exclusion of everything else, often harming their own personal growth and external relationships.

Codependent relationships can be one of the most difficult, but often most necessary, relationships to leave. An interdependent relationship is when you *want* your partner rather than *need* them, like the codependent partner does. A codependent relationship is unbalanced because of the incompleteness one feels without the other, a feeling that goes beyond loving someone into an inability to function without them. Codependent relationships are incredibly difficult to leave because you are both so entangled in one another—no other form of living seems to make sense or even feels feasible. There is a fear present that you or your partner will not be able to survive without one another.

Clear signs of a codependent relationship include only spending your time with them, canceling other plans without a second thought to be with them, feeling afraid to set boundaries or ask for space in your relationship, or feeling overwhelmed when you're without them. Often there will be partner roles, such as one person taking on the role of saving the other: one person trying to save the other from something external (an unloving family, a traumatic experience, or other difficult life circumstances), or even from themselves (in the form of self-destructive behavior). These relationships often rest on an unhealthy need to save or be saved, making it much more complicated to bring them to a healthy place.

As with anything, I won't say it is impossible. If you feel uncertain about your relationship, set new boundaries for yourself. Try not answering your partner's texts from all hours of the night, or making plans with friends and sticking to them. Your partner's responses to these new changes will reveal the nature of your dynamic. Just because you two may be codependent doesn't mean either of you are bad people—it's just the way you two have ended up forming a dynamic together. Sometimes two good people who love one another can still end up feeding into each other's pain.

Still, once you know your relationship needs to end, even the awareness of being unhappy is not always enough to ease the pains of leaving. Guilt and fear will stir, and especially in codependent relationships, you may resent yourself for causing your partner pain, or even fear their resentment of you. If you were friends before dating, consciously choosing to detach from that person who you met however long ago is difficult. Your friend group could unravel with this new rift; you might fear that your friends will be forced to take sides, and that isn't an irrational thing to be worried about. This division is natural as your friends choose loyalty to you or your partner, although this doesn't always last forever, and your friend group in school is bound to change anyway. It's hard to let go of the way things were, but the changes don't have to hurt either.

Returning to the thought of how your partner would react if you left them, recall the relentlessness of love. Under pain people can be cruel. It is to be expected, depending on the partner, that tactics—harmful ones, false ones—will be used. An especially unstable partner may threaten you with their own physical safety, making you seem like the only way to ensure their well-being. This is clear cut emotional manipulation, and it's easy to fall for. Be realistic with yourself though: your partner is not a child needing to be watched over, nor are they a bird with their wings clipped. They have gone their entire life prior to you surviving just fine. They may be hurting, but they are a capable person. The guilt of breaking up with someone is immense, but it's not selfish to leave a relationship that is hurting you. Don't be held back by what you feel is the *sensible* thing to do. No part of love is sensible.

Maintain your standards. We get used to the functionality of our relationships, healthy or not. Our way of life is modified to who we are with them, new patterns develop with our partner. One of the most challenging aspects of breaking up is going back to life without them. Don't settle. Don't accept something that's not worth your time just because you fear being alone. Pain is stimulating. Deceptively, it often feels indistinguishable from love. An easy justification for toxicity is that even though the bad is really bad, the good is so so good, because it's intoxicating, because it is sweet honey that seeps into you, slowly, relentlessly. The anxiety and stress is entertaining to your brain, occupying your nervous system, never leaving room for a dull moment. We choose the love we think we deserve. When we are so used to chaos, peace feels more like a lack. If you have been taught insecurity and shame, any time your relationship has a problem, you believe it's your fault. It feels toxic but if you just *got it together* everything would be fine.

Remember: a relationship takes two. If there are issues, that means it's a result of both of you. It may be that one person is allowing their partner to treat them poorly, but that in itself is permission to create a problem. Remind yourself of your own worth. Do you deserve the treatment you're receiving? Does your partner deserve the treatment they're receiving? You have full freedom in choosing your relationship. Is this the one you want to be in? Is there a possibility there is someone out there that will treat you better? If you're having to ask yourself these questions, here's a hint. The answer: without a doubt.

Knowing if you're supposed to stay in your relationship takes time, but beneath the many layers of things you may consider and reconsider, you do know. There will be hints that you feel out of place. If you are asked about your relationship and you find yourself justifying it not only to the one who questioned it, but to yourself, the answer is always within reach. If your real friends start questioning how happy you truly are with your partner, start questioning it yourself. In the rush of dating, your good friends can often see things that aren't clear to you. They can see how you're changing in ways that are no longer apparent to you.

Letting go of a partner is an act of surrender. Even when breaking up is your choice and an act of empowerment, it still requires a surrendering of the known, a vault into uncertainty. You must relinquish control over them and your relationship in order to take control over your own life again. It stings thinking about what they will do after you, who they will be with, not being able to talk to them the same way anymore. Nevertheless, you both will move on. If you weren't happy together, your lives can only keep getting better apart, but in order to find that you must let go. There are eight billion people in this world. If you want to find someone, you will.

CHAPTER 12: THE BREAKUP

An end is only a beginning. Just as nature has to shed what has decayed in the fall in order to grow anew in the spring, there may come a season when you'll need to shake off anyone or anything impeding your own growth. Regardless of cause or execution, it will hurt. In the midst of a breakup, this reminder will almost certainly feel trivial, but it's important to commend your personal bravery. You choose the best life for yourself by letting go of an unhealthy relationship. Any time you make that choice, acknowledge that you're taking care of yourself in ways many people are too afraid to. Be proud of your fortitude.

The key to closure in a break up is to stay authentic. Do not circumvent your own resolution. When having the breakup conversation with your partner, do not sugar coat anything. Be clear and firm in your decision. This statement is not to be interpreted as "tear their heart out and step on it" (as tempting as that may be when in pain), but rather be genuine in describing your reasons for leaving the relationship. Avoiding the screaming, heavy blaming, and profanities. Kindly but firmly explain why it isn't working for you. Own your part of the breakup as well—remember a relationship takes two. If it didn't work out, both of you contributed to that fall, even if just by allowing something to continue. Most people deserve to know why it's ending, but putting the other person aside, if you don't say everything you feel, you'll end up coming back to them just to let out your unsaid pains. You'll be unable to release yourself from the relationship due to the immutable arguments you'll be having with them inside your head. In simpler terms, if you can't face them, you'll end up fighting yourself instead.

Intimidating as it may be, if possible, break up in person. Breaking up over the phone is a comfortable way to avoid owning your decision. No matter how undoubtedly valid your reasons are for leaving, not doing it face-to-face doesn't allow you to empower yourself as you should. The urge to make decisions in the safety of your own space is a right you have. However, if you cannot be upfront about this choice with another person, have you truly embraced your own well-being? On the other side of things, you may be anticipating that your partner is going to break up with you soon. Perhaps they're even telling you that you need to have an "important conversation" and you're beginning to feel the end creeping up. As frightening as it is, don't run from it. Respect the action they're taking and let them take it.

To respect both yourself and your partner, don't make a show of your breakup. Avoid telling them it's over in front of a big crowd of people. If you do want a show, reevaluate your motivations. As breakups usually include a meaningful conversation, having it go down in front of your friends is messy and unproductive for the two of you. If you have an emotionally or physically abusive or manipulative partner, of course it's also fair to be thoughtful about where you choose to break up with them. The location and method of breaking up shouldn't infringe upon your well-being. Generally though, a breakup—no matter how amiable or how bitter it is—is a difficult experience you two are facing together. Most people do not deserve to be humiliated in this process, so the atmosphere you create while breaking up with them is both a sign of your acknowledgement of and empathy for them. Being able to show kindness when you are in pain is the bravest thing you can do.

Once you both have had the opportunity to speak, set your boundaries. When you feel what is being said is no longer pertinent or productive, you can say that the conversation is done. The weight of pain from a break up pushes us into anger. What gets said in the heat of the moment isn't always something we really mean. Sometimes it's better to end the conversation sooner before you both hurt each other even further. If you made this decision for your own well-being but they're responding violently to you, you don't have to listen any further. You've made the decision to break up and you're no longer responsible for their feelings or any conversation regarding them.

Before having the conversation, remind yourself that in this pain, they may do anything they can to talk you out of leaving them. Stay strong in your decision: don't be wavered by tears, screaming, or gaslighting. It's not to say that your partner isn't genuinely hurting, they may not even be trying to manipulate you, but keep trusting yourself. It's okay to walk away, it's better for you both in the long run. There is no harm done in choosing your own peace.

I wish I could promise that the day you break up is the one that will take the most strength, but it isn't. For the next couple weeks, months, or even a whole year, it will take strength. You may not even feel it the first day. In the beginning you may feel full with nothing at all but a sweet relief. Right after breaking off an unhealthy relationship you are suffused in liberating adrenaline, inoculating you with your freedom now returned. That same feeling of euphoria can be our bodies protecting us from the discomfort of a breakup. The second day can be much more difficult for some people; everything sets in and they realize that their life is now altered in perpetuity. Even (and especially) a good decision can be the most painful one. That said, you may respond very differently. The first day could feel the most heartbreaking and if that's the case, don't try to run from the pain.

No matter how long or short your relationship was, or what kind of commitment you had to one another, it was still a chapter of your life. As much as you may want to move on, those feelings are still real ones. The pain is inevitable, and delaying the feeling only prolongs this tender adjustment period.

After the initial feelings set in, there are generally five main stages of a breakup. They are: denial, rage and intensity, negotiating and resisting, depression and isolation, and finally acceptance and contentment. The pendulum of your emotions swings tentatively between these conflicting feelings. These shifts can feel overwhelming, leaving you wanting clarity and a sense of control. Thus, understanding this process amidst all of the confusion will help you make more conscious and ultimately more healthy choices for yourself.

The first stage is typically denial. Denial is our system's reaction to keep us safe when the shock of a relationship ending may otherwise be too much to bear. Your feelings of being completely overwhelmed and even confused make you unable to come to terms with the fact that it's over. In your mind it cannot be reality that you two are done, so you're gripped onto your phone anticipating and hoping for a text message from them. And in many cases you'll receive one, but that doesn't mean you should respond.

In an attempt to savor your bond, one or both of you may opt for staying friends. Don't stay friends—at least, not at first. This is only a form of denial. As tempting and possible as it may feel, it's futile. I can nearly guarantee that one person has or will try to fish something else out of the relationship. On the off chance neither does, one of you is likely to feel jealous and may be unable to fully move on to a new partner. Even if you can, your new partner will probably feel uncomfortable with you being friends with an ex. From every point of view, some part of the relationship is being latched onto that it is now time to release. I cannot speak to the intentions of you or your ex-partner, but be aware of your own true motivations for staying friends. If you and your ex share such a bond that can expand beyond the romantic, wait a couple months, at least, to become friends. Give and take space. You both need time to breathe and process. Release your grip on any sentimental objects you may have from them. If throwing them away feels too extreme, designate a box for everything and put it in a place you cannot see. Removing reminders of your ex-partner takes a lot of strength, but staying in an environment that feels like them won't let you move on.

Eventually the full realization will settle in, bringing with it a sudden intensity. In this second stage, that intensity will manifest for most of us in the same way: rage. You'll begin to think, "How dare they," and what follows that statement will vary for us all. If you go to school with them and they seem unbothered by the whole thing or more than happy walking around, don't pay it too much mind. Everyone grieves and copes in ways we're not aware of, and the excessive smiles may be their way of trying to be okay. Even if they are as carefree as they seem, their emotions are no longer relevant to your life: it's best to focus on your own. If you ended the relationship, you've made the decision to separate them from your life. Respect yourself for taking that action by no longer making them a priority in your life.

Rebounding. In the midst of the intense emotions in this second stage, the idea itself is seductive—it is skilled in seducing you away from the emptiness you are feeling now that you're without your partner. That is exactly what it is doing though: taking you away, shielding you. Avoidance. When the idea feels so intriguing you can barely resist, consider this: Why can't I survive on my own? Can I not be alone with this pain, am I not strong enough to feel it? These questions are direct and harsh, but drowning your emotions in anything else is more harm done. Allowing yourself to instead inhabit the small, fragile feeling of a breakup takes more strength than blurring it with a new source of adrenaline. If you are constantly bouncing around from person to person, you will never be able to trust yourself to be alone.

Your pain and anger may cause you to want to make them hurt like you're hurting, to make sure that they have to feel like you have to feel, to show them all they lost. Enacting revenge, even in the smallest ways, only proves your unwillingness to let go. It is not a testament to your strength, but a symbol of their hold on you. Resist the urge to wear specific outfits to make them jealous, don't post a photo to make them see what they're missing or hang out with the people you know they didn't like you being around. Put on a nice outfit to show *yourself* your worth, go out to a concert to make *yourself* feel good about being alive, but don't broadcast it for them. If the intention behind your actions is to put them down, you're still attached. You are still doing things for them, not for yourself. It's normal to feel furious and to wish they could be in pain, but channel that into bettering yourself. When you're pissed off, go back to the gym, use the anger to drive you to finish an assignment or pursue something you've been thinking about. Convert the pain into productivity and it will help you release it. Just being angry is okay too. Scream into a pillow, vent, shatter something of glass, feel everything without holding back. Curse the world out so you can be friends with it again.

Following the end of one of my relationships, I decided to pick up hiking—a routine which meant an alarm to wake me up at 4:30 in the morning, and again at 4:45 in case I didn't wake up for the first one. In the beginning, I'd go every morning in an attempt to be faster and more disciplined than the soon rising sun. 4:30am: Put on clothes, grab the dog, don't be too loud so as to disturb Mom and Dad. I wanted to be mentally tough. I wanted the stamina and the strength which came with headache-inducing, half-awake trudging through fields uphill. I wanted to be up before everyone else and regain all of the confidence in myself I had just lost. If I could wake up and burn through my tired calves, I had won before anyone else got the chance to.

This type of discipline is admirable. It *does* strengthen your mental, as well as your physical, fortitude. It *did* make me feel more confident in myself, but what it also did was mean I never slept. I'd spend all night in my thoughts or schoolwork (which

I was falling behind in due to the lack of sleep from my hiking adventures), and then wake up a few hours later to beat the rest of the world to the top of the hill. I stopped eating as much or showing up for my teammates during after-school practice because I was so exhausted from the start of my day. It *was* a good idea, it just wasn't the time for it. The sleep deprivation not only didn't put me ahead of everyone else since I was so tired, it also didn't make me forget how insecure I had felt after I had been broken up with. It was a routine driven by anger, an emotion that was perfectly understandable for me to be feeling. However I wish now I had chosen something softer and more nurturing (such as weekend hikes during my leisure time), that allowed me to burn off anger and regain my relationship with myself, without sacrificing another part of my life.

After moving through the anger you reach the third phase: negotiating and resisting. The adrenaline subsides and sadness starts to seep in through the cracks. You'll probably have some sort of an *enlightened* realization that "you've made a mistake" and your brain will filter out the bad parts of the relationship so you only remember the happy memories. You'll think about the intimacy, dates, romantic gestures, perfect moments, and you'll have this itching feeling that you just let go of your one true love. I'll let you in on a stark but comforting secret: everyone feels like that. This is the time to remember your boundaries and sink back into the feeling of self-trust. Don't text, call, or meet up with your ex to share your newfound perspective on the breakup. Many people find it easier to move on by blocking or unfriending their ex-partners online. If your ex sets this boundary, don't find new ways to contact them. They are processing the end in their own way and don't have an obligation to have any more conversations with you that they don't want to. Don't try to reach them through loopholes of prolonged eye contact or purposely being where they will be. When all you can do is feel, try to force yourself to break it down logically. Why wouldn't it have worked? Why is it better that it is over? In the case that you ended the relationship, respect and reflect on your decision. Why did I decide it would be healthier for me to leave? Was I truly happy and fulfilled in the relationship? What was hurting me that made me make that decision? What do I need to start doing to get back on track? Who can I reconnect with during this hard time in my life—what are my resources?

Trying to understand why your relationship ended can feel overwhelming in this stage, so consider seeking guidance from someone you trust. Have a close friend or family member help you acknowledge the truth about your relationship. Your mind will lie to you, it will sweeten the bitter aspects of your relationship because it is more comfortable than overcoming the pain of letting go. Kathy B. Overman, a respected clinical therapist specializing in relationship issues and trauma, once said, "Your nervous system will always choose a familiar hell over an unfamiliar heaven." An outside perspective from someone you trust can provide a much needed dose of clarity when you're in this fragile state.

Say that you were the one who got broken up with. Consider why that is. When you really reflect on your relationship, is this a healthier decision for them? How were you both affected by and affecting each other? Is there anything you need to take accountability for? Accept that there were flaws in the relationship and work to understand what they were. The more insight you're able to gain, the better equipped you'll be to make your next relationship a truly loving and fulfilling one. While all these questions are helpful, perhaps the most important one you can ask yourself when you're the one that's been broken up with is, "Why would I want to be with someone who doesn't want to be with me?" If the relationship ended through no fault of your own and without mutual understanding, if your partner feels anything less than a strong desire to be with you through it all, they aren't the one for you. There's undoubtedly a better match out there, someone who will love and appreciate everything you are, and you are freeing yourself up to find them.

When it comes to talking after a breakup, the less the better. If you've tried to break off communication with your ex and they won't stop reaching out, don't reply. One of you has made a decision to end this and for the sake of you both, stay separated. Whether it's a huge apology, angry messages or kind ones, you've both set a boundary that they're crossing. If you decide to open the message you'll get pulled back into the dynamic of the relationship. It may appear like they've changed but realistically, they couldn't have changed in the week or month since you've broken up. Not to disregard the possibility of them changing at all, but it will take more time than that.

———————————————————————————

—

As the weeks and months pass, the pain of no contact with someone who used to be so important to you can become life sucking. You'll likely enter the fourth phase, depression and isolation, in which It feels as though you can't gather the life force to move, work, or eat. The things you love will feel irrelevant, socializing with your friends may not matter to you at all anymore. Here's the part where you don't feel like you can be strong anymore.

To this I say, let yourself be soft. Slow down. Feel it. However, don't get stuck. Grant yourself a time limit to your mourning. Commit to letting yourself do nothing for, let's say, eight days, and then get back into life. Force yourself to eat when you don't want to. Be kind to yourself. Take a hot shower, do something that makes you feel good. Make yourself exercise and see the people who care about you. Surrounding yourself with those closest to you will help fill the gap left by your ex. It will be a lonely period, but don't reminisce about them. The box where you placed all the belongings that remind you of them should stay shut. Take yourself off social media so you don't see what they're doing, it's only salt in the wound. Looking at social media at all will make things harder. Social media is designed to fool you into thinking they've moved on—the sad, depressing videos on your feed are curated by the algorithm to reflect your own sadness. Always remember that social media is just an app that wants your attention, not a mirror of reality.

The final stage of a breakup is acceptance. It's time to come to terms with the end and allow yourself to shift into your next beginning. Acceptance takes time, and reaching this point may take months and you may be in different phases of this stage for many months more. As life goes on and you see your ex moving on and evolving, you'll have to constantly be accepting reality. To reach the point of contentment and peace with your life again, you must remember who you are. What do you love to do, what makes you excited and riled up? What are the qualities you love about yourself? Throw yourself into relearning your own value and worth. Now is a time of reflection and realization.

Some questions you should begin asking yourself:

1. Who was I in the relationship? Was I my authentic self?
2. Did I like who I became in the relationship?
3. Why did I attract someone like that into my life? Do I have a pattern?
4. What did I learn about myself in that relationship?
5. Where do I need to take responsibility in the relationship?
6. What do I want to be different next time?
7. Was I happy?
8. What did I love about the relationship?
9. What hurt me in the relationship?
10. Was it really love or a different type of bond?

While reflecting on this list, take a look at the one I asked you to write in Chapter 4. Are the values on your list the same now as they were before your relationship ended? Are there some things there that are still definitely non-negotiable? Did you discover that you don't actually want some of the things you had originally written? Perhaps nothing has changed, or perhaps everything has changed. Every relationship provides us with an opportunity to learn more about ourselves. Develop a different way of looking at the end; embrace and change your perspective, recognize the rushing nature of young relationships and try to be grateful for the experience.

It is the spirit of such pain to become cynical to love, but don't let it take hold. Instead, bring laughter to any thought that "love is fake and dead." We all think about it at some point, and sometimes, amid the pain and distress, we have to laugh at the dark feelings that accompany it. We've only experienced a small part of what relationships and life will be like. Still, of course, just because a relationship is temporary doesn't mean it lacks meaning —and most relationships, by nature, are temporary. Everyone we grow close to offers us a new perspective on life. We get a chance to experience this world in different colors and tones. Every experience we have is important and if we experience this life next to one person, that's just as meaningful. The point of being here is to interact with and love each other. Our ability to share these different forms of love is part of the human gift.

Yet even though we know this, the end always catches us off guard. There's a kind of beauty in the rise and fall—it's part of the cycle of life. Because love isn't just in the staying. It's in the trying, the feeling, the remembering.

To see someone in their most difficult moments and still recognize who they are at their core—that they are precious, that we all began as children, that we have all been hurt. To remember these things—not to excuse their mistakes, but to meet them wholeheartedly, without ignorance—that is love.

CHAPTER 13: TWO CONFESSIONS AND A PROMISE

T he first confession: I wrote this book during, what was known to me at that moment in time, as the most difficult breakup of my life. Most days I didn't want to write. The words felt more like my soul bleeding onto the paper. Reflecting now, that is what it was, I think: a death, followed by a tentative and demanding stroll through hell, and subsequently a rebirth. A necessary rebirth, at that. While writing this book, for the most part, it couldn't be objective. Love and loss, by their very nature, are subjective matters—our views on them can't help but be influenced by our feelings and experiences. Because of that, in order to make this book as authentic as it could possibly be, I had to face my feelings and experiences head on. I had to tear down everything that was protecting me from my love and my loss. Of course, when it comes to matters of the heart, logic can only take us so far. Love often overrides reason, and despite everything I know, there were many days when I felt completely broken. I admit this to you so can be in comfort with the fact that, no matter how much awareness or grasp you have on the mechanics of healthy relationships, sometimes it still just hurts like hell.

A second confession: Over the time it took me to write this

book I began becoming more and more conflicted over what I was writing. This is in part because I have been actively learning so much more as I have continued to live my life during this process —but also because I began to wonder what the point of writing this was. More specifically, I didn't know if, by deeply analyzing and breaking down love and human connection, I was taking away the focus of the very point of it. Is not the point of love to simply love? Or is that speculation of my own cynicism just another form of my fear in my relationships?

When you're falling into or pulling yourself back out of a relationship, most of the things I say in this book will certainly exit your memory. If you are to keep just one thing with you, I hope it's this: when all feels lost, when the ruined relationships pile one on top of the other and you begin to think life cannot possibly get better, have hope. Have ferocious, unwavering hope. There is so much you do not yet know is out there, so much waiting for you to discover. Unrevealed loves, adventures, joys, laughter, and still more heartbreaks. You cannot see it, you cannot touch it, it's incomprehensible, for now, but there is more to come. I am nothing if not averse to making promises, but I promise you that life has more in store for you. Just keep looking forward. Have faith in the unknown and trust in yourself to make it there.

We are all human, bound to love and fated to an enduring lack of permanence in our lives. We all have a story that has taught us how to maneuver our way through this life. We all learn, and in order to learn we all must make mistakes. You won't get anything I've written here right on the first try. I'm still trying to get it right. The only thing you can do is keep going: keep trying, keep learning. Think of this book as your guide, a cheat code so to say. Listen to your heart, not that I could stop you, but go about your relationships with this new knowledge so that the bonds you form will be even more incredible. And, keep having fun with it, take love with lightness. Enjoy every moment wholeheartedly and know, if it's time to move on, that there is more beauty to come.

Outside of yourself, remember the common world. We in this generation have access to a common mind. Social media is something we instinctively spend most of our free time in, but if you really think about why that is you'll find that the gift it *can* bring us is much greater than we typically think. Think about how many influencers you see talking or reels you send your friends because they are funny and relatable. Think about how millions of other people from all around the globe are liking and sharing those very same videos. People from different countries, families, religions; people with different values, political stances, sexualities; people who look different, who talk differently, who see the world differently. All of these people are looking at the same thing you are and thinking, "Hey, I feel like that too." A stranger created that video because they felt those emotions or wanted that car or thought that dog was cute—and millions of other strangers are liking it because they are thinking the same thing.

When we really become aware of that concept we can start to *use* that to come together. We don't need to care for one another with compassion and empathy because we are romantically connected, part of the same family or in the same class. We can care for one another because, even in a ten second clip online, we are all humans seeking joy and community. We all need to look at each other and first think about our similarities before our differences. If we can look at the person we love and choose to treat them with kindness, there is no reason we cannot do that to strangers. We need to be able to look at the people around us and first make the assumption that we know nothing about them, but *share* something in common with them before we assume we know something about them and share nothing with them.

No matter where we come from, we all seek love. We all seek partnership and knowing. What separates us is a lack of instinctive empathy. There is a hope for beauty in all of our own lives. One step at a time, we can get more curious about how we may see and build that beauty with each other.

ACKNOWLEDGEMENTS

I would like to express my deepest gratitude to the following people and places that have made this book possible:

To my family, whose unwavering support has been my foundation throughout this journey. Your belief in me has been a constant source of strength.

To my friends, who reminded me often to take life a little less seriously, and to enjoy the experience of writing a book.

To Wilson's Cafe in Connecticut, a quiet and welcoming space that offered me comfort and inspiration during countless writing sessions. Thank you for being my second home.

To my debate coach, Coach K, whose mentorship and guidance have shaped my voice and perspective. Your dedication to teaching me how to think critically and speak with confidence has left an indelible mark on me.

To my high school English teachers, who cultivated my love for language and storytelling. Your passion for literature and teaching has been an invaluable influence.

To the beautiful women from the I Know A Place community, whose embodiment of feminine empowerment and representation has inspired me to embrace my own voice and strength. Your example has shown me what it means to stand proudly in who we are.

And to all the incredible people I've met along this journey— those who cheered me on, those who were behind the scenes, those who listened to my ideas, and those who got excited on my behalf about the work I'm doing. You kept my passion alive and reminded me why this matters. Your belief in me helped keep my fire burning.

Thank you all for your support, encouragement, and the love you've shown me along the way.

ABOUT THE AUTHOR

Charley Sky Gardner

As a teen author, Charley Sky (affectionately known as "Sky") focuses on guiding young people through the complexities of relationships and love, offering a fresh perspective rooted in lived experience. She is dedicated to empowering others to understand themselves.

Raised in Los Angeles, Charley Sky is now a junior at a New England boarding school, a highly impactful activist for organizations for homeless youth (YAC and Ignite Food Project, Bali), and fluent in Mandarin Chinese.

She is passionate about strengthening human connection and fostering conscious and expansive connections through her writing, visual art, poetry and way of living.

www.ingramcontent.com/pod-product-compliance
Lightning Source LLC
LaVergne TN
LVHW041228080426
835508LV00011B/1116